# LAND IN
# CONFLICT

# LAND IN CONFLICT

SEAN NOLON
ONA FERGUSON
PAT FIELD

With a foreword by
Bruce Babbitt

Managing
and Resolving
Land Use
Disputes

LINCOLN INSTITUTE
OF LAND POLICY
CAMBRIDGE, MASSACHUSETTS

*Library of Congress Cataloging-in-Publication Data*
Nolon, Sean.
  Land in conflict : managing and resolving land use disputes / Sean Nolon, Ona Ferguson, and Pat Field.
     pages cm
  Includes bibliographical references and index.
  ISBN 978-1-55844-246-7 (alk. paper)
  1. Land use—United States.   2. Land use—United States—Planning.   3. Land tenure—United States.  4. City planning—United States.  I. Ferguson, Ona.  II. Field, Patrick, 1963–   III. Title.
  HD205.N65 2013
  333.73'130973—dc23

                           2013009836

*Designed by Westchester Publishing Services*

Composed in Chaparral Pro by Westchester Publishing Services in Danbury, Connecticut. Printed and bound by Puritan Press Inc., in Hollis, New Hampshire.

♻ The paper is Rolland Enviro100, an acid-free, 100 percent PCW recycled sheet.

MANUFACTURED IN THE UNITED STATES OF AMERICA

# ■ CONTENTS

# ■ ILLUSTRATIONS

*Photos*

# ■ FOREWORD

In 1993, when I arrived in Washington as secretary of the interior, a small gray songbird called the California gnatcatcher also arrived to become my instructor in land use planning. It came about when I placed the bird on the Endangered Species List.

That listing had far-reaching consequences. It became a federal crime to disturb or destroy even an acre of the remaining habitat utilized by the birds. What I had not fully comprehended was that the remaining populations of these endangered birds needed a lot of space in which to nest and forage, including several hundred thousand acres of prime development land stretching from Los Angeles south to the Mexican border.

All that land was now off-limits to development. As subdivision and highway construction came to a halt, developers headed to the Congress, demanding repeal of the act. My colleagues at the White House, pressing me for a solution, were quick to remind me that the president would undoubtedly be running for re-election and would need California's 54 electoral votes.

After assessing our options, it appeared the only way to lift the development moratorium would be by working out a region-wide land use plan that would allow development to proceed—provided we could guarantee permanent protection for enough of the remaining habitat to ensure the survival of the gnatcatcher populations. Developers would have to concede a lot of land to the bird in exchange for the green light to move forward with their subdivisions and roads.

Out came the maps, and they did not offer much encouragement. The coastal habitat of the bird was fragmented into thousands of irregular parcels scattered across three counties. To design and establish connected preserves responsive not to survey lines but to ecological needs of the bird seemed an insurmountable task.

A federally led negotiation affecting thousands of landowners, hundreds of subdividers, and dozens of environmental groups in three counties was out of the question. Land use decisions must be grounded at the local level, with state and federal actors playing a complementary role in shaping decisions. We would therefore have to reach out, delegating authority and responsibility to state government, which could in turn delegate down to county and municipal governments that could deal with landowners in the familiar context of local planning and zoning regulations.

The first task was to structure a negotiation process to draw in representatives at all levels of government, developers, environmentalists, and civic leaders. Fortunately, we encountered a progressive state government ready to engage in the process, led by Doug Wheeler, the resources secretary. On the ground level, San Diego County became the test case with strong leadership provided by the mayor of San Diego, Susan Golding, and her staff. From there on we would, by trial and error, learn many of the lessons so insightfully discussed in this book.

Next we had to identify other stakeholders and encourage their strongest leaders to join in. On one end of the spectrum were environmental advocates arguing that releasing any land for development would further diminish the chance for survival of the bird population. At the other end, developers and landowners saw a huge infringement on their legally protected property rights.

The next challenge was to broaden the discussion beyond zero-sum confines and to introduce new and often unconventional ideas that were ongoing in multiple forums. A major hurdle would be economic: ensuring that landowners would receive fair value for any land necessary to fill out the preserves. But how could we compensate owners of ecologically essential landholdings while exacting some contribution from other landowners outside the planned preserves?

Transferable development rights and the use of conservation ease-ments could assist large landowners. In other cases, particularly with smaller landowners, outright purchase would be the better alternative. A few enterprising groups initiated mitigation banking, purchasing critical habitat land, and recouping the investment by selling mitigation credits to developers. The San Diego Zoo, with a wide base of support in the community, proved an especially important advocate for the program.

In an undertaking of this size, federal, state, and local appropriations were essential to complete the open space preserves. To secure public funds meant building political support, which in turn required an expan-sive communications plan explaining the process and stressing the mutual benefits accruing to the entire community in the form of open space, wildlife enhancement, and watershed protection, thereby increasing property values and making San Diego City and County a more attractive place in which to live and work.

After several years of negotiation and compromise, the plan went into effect; the details can still be visited on the websites of the City and County of San Diego. A land use undertaking of this scope and complexity could hardly have been imagined, much less achieved, through traditional adversarial procedures driven by the prospects of litigation and judicial intervention. Land use issues, large and small alike, almost always have implications for the broader community, which should lead to more frequent use of the techniques that are the subject of this book.

—*Bruce Babbitt*
*Fellow, Blue Moon Fund*
*Board Member, Lincoln Institute of Land Policy*

# ■ PREFACE

Why do some decisions about land use go smoothly while others generate multiple lawsuits, ruin relationships, and waste community resources? This book focuses on those land use disputes that take so much of our time and usually produce unsatisfying results. The disputes we explore involve zoning, planning, and development decisions that arise at the local level, but often have implications at the state and national levels. While the principal decision makers are local governments, state and federal agencies are frequently involved in these decisions.

Depending on the state, "local" may refer to the town, township, village, or county level of government. Local disputes are generally site-specific and influence residential, commercial, and industrial neighbors. Though land use decisions often include environmental issues (such as wetlands, water quality, storm water, and flooding), our focus is not primarily on environmental cases.

Through our years of experience and drawing from conflict theory in other fields, we have developed an approach to minimize the destructive nature of many significant local land use conflicts. This approach encourages parties to focus on mutual interests and strive to achieve mutual gains.

Throughout the book, we use stories to illustrate our approach. Many of these cases are real, in addition to one hypothetical case (the Discordia Mall). The cases illustrate how mutual gains approaches can be utilized and give insight into how these approaches might play out on the ground. Many of the techniques highlighted in these cases originate from the collaborative practices used by mediators. Accordingly, mediation theory and practice serve as ongoing concepts in our approach.

At the core of this approach is the reality that communities have many choices about how to handle controversial land use decisions. However, many leaders believe they have no choice or voice in land use decisions, since decisions about regulating the use of land must follow specific procedures codified in state and local laws. Yet these legal requirements serve only as procedural minimums and do not preclude the addition of more collaborative forms of decision making. A community may elect to use the required, minimal procedure or it can elect to implement a supplemental process that enhances the interaction between the stake-holders involved. Some communities even choose to incorporate the collaborative processes of the mutual gains approach into their bylaws and ordinances.

The approach in this book is built on sound practices at the core of planning theory. The website of the American Planning Association (APA) lists the "ability to function as a mediator or facilitator when community interests conflict" as one of the skills of successful planners. In addition, the APA's guidebook on planning for smart growth, *Growing Smart,* notes the importance of collaborative decision making in the context of planning and development approvals. Chapter 7 on local planning bemoans the fact that most state planning statutes do little to promote dialogue and to advocate for citizen involvement in comprehensive planning (Meck 2002). Only a few states— Florida, Maine, Washington, Oregon, and the District of Columbia—have adopted statutes that encourage more dialogue and collaboration in planning decisions. Chapter 10 provides a model ordinance provision to allow aggrieved parties to mediate instead of filing a legal appeal. Chapter 8 on effective development provides guidance for nonjudicial mediation and for the review of decisions. The Urban Land Institute's book entitled *Breaking the Development Logjam: New Strategies for Building Community Support* (Porter 2006) explains how to enhance citizen participation and collaborative decision making. Our book builds on those suggestions by describing a comprehensive approach to managing and resolving controversial local land use disputes.

Why would a community choose to supplement or improve its minimal, land use decision-making process? How would adding more steps solve difficult problems? Would this create more work, take more time, and cause more delays?

Consider how the required process recently worked in controversial land use decisions in your community. Was the result satisfying to a range of stakeholders? Was the process rewarding? Were relationships improved? Did participants share valuable information about the community? Did the process contribute to the growth of the community? Chances are that few people were happy with the results, the process was long and expensive, long-standing relationships were stressed, the information shared was incomplete, and the sense of community was compromised.

If citizens and government acknowledge that the existing process can be adversarial and stifle creativity, they are more likely to seek out and participate in more constructive approaches. State and county governments can help local governments transition to a new approach by providing training and education for local boards. Some regional planning commissions, bar associations, state and federal agencies, and civic groups already provide this kind of training for local leaders. The Land Use Leadership Alliance in the Hudson River Valley and the Alberta Municipal Assistance Program in Canada are examples of regionally funded land use dispute resolution and education programs. In addition, groups like the American Planning Association, the Urban Land Institute, and the Lincoln Institute of Land Policy have programs and materials to help raise awareness among local officials.

The approach laid out in this book will help local planners, lawyers, developers, residents, and students devise strategies to address high-conflict in complex land use cases. The types of disputes appropriate for the mutual gains approach have the following characteristics.

- There will be long-term, far-reaching impacts on the community or landscape.
- The board has some discretion in decision making.
- Numerous stakeholders are affected or have expressed an interest in the project.
- There will likely be a challenge to an outcome if it is not developed collaboratively.

This book is written as a primer for those involved in controversial land use decisions. Local planners can obtain advice and ideas to address the problems they face. Proponents of projects, both developers and their financiers, may consider how to incorporate these approaches into their projects and plans. This book can also inform the public and give them the insights to request that local decision makers and project proponents utilize these principles, steps, and processes to improve the public's access to and involvement in land use decisions. Finally, this book can serve as a reference guide and an introduction to students interested in land use, including the next generation of attorneys, planners, and site engineers.

# PART I ▪ BASICS

# CHAPTER 1

■ □ □ □ □ □ □ □ □

# The Mutual Gains Approach to Resolving Land Use Disputes

In the United States, over 25,000 local and regional governments play a role in making land use decisions. Every day, local officials must make challenging decisions involving land that impact open space, economic development, transportation, and countless other issues. These decisions affect the built environment, the landscape, and the economy for decades or even centuries. How officials make these decisions influences the way community members interact with one another and whether they work as a cohesive or a divided group.

To help understand how a land use decision process can affect an outcome, we have created the fictional town of Discordia, where a dilapidated 1960s strip mall sits on a three-acre parcel of land. As shown in figure 1.1, the parcel with the vacant Discordia Mall fronts on a busy four-lane road, is across the street from a gas station and a supermarket, is flanked by a bank and a small office building, is close to a newly restored creek on one side, and in the back corner adjoins a school in a residential neighborhood. The owners of the mall have proposed demolishing the existing one-story building to erect two new, three-story buildings with commercial space on the ground floor and two floors of offices above.

This may seem like a major improvement for the town, but that is not the initial reaction of the public. Parents of children at the adjacent Quimby Elementary School have expressed the most heated concern, raising questions and anxieties about increased traffic, danger from delivery trucks, and the general safety of children in the neighborhood. Residents of the neighboring apartment complex are worried about traffic, odors from garbage, lighting on the buildings and parking lot, hours of operation, and noise. A local environmental group trying to restore adjacent Discordia Creek has expressed outrage that the new development

3

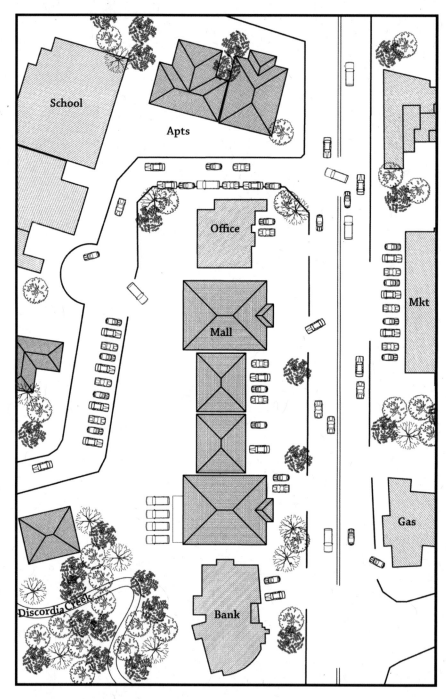

**FIGURE 1.1  Map of Proposed Discordia Mall**
Drawn by Martha Paynter.

would add impervious surfaces on the bank of the recently restored stream habitat. A group of parents has written an editorial stating that the project is out of scale and would threaten their children's health, asking the planning board not to approve the project. Another article voices concern about the competition this new complex would present to nearby businesses. Several rumors have begun to circulate about the poor reputation of the developer and the possible corruption of municipal officials.

The developer is concerned about losing money if the proposal for a conditional use permit (a zoning mechanism that identifies certain uses that are appropriate under the right conditions) is delayed by community opposition. The municipality is troubled by the vocal outcry from local residents. Hearings are postponed so the town may collect further information. Citizens feel that their questions are not being answered or their concerns addressed. Local board members, all volunteers, are disheartened that this is becoming such a difficult, time-consuming, and contentious job. Formerly friendly neighbors glare at each other at their kids' soccer games. The decision is at a standstill and everyone is unhappy.

Unfortunately, this example is common across the United States in small towns and large cities alike. Take just a few examples of headlines collected from across the country:

- "Mormon Church's Plans for Land Upset Harlem." *New York Times*, 9 January 2012.
- "Two Groups Opposing Walmart Neighborhood Market Zoning Case in Fort Worth." *Fort Worth Star-Telegram*, 9 January 2012.
- "City Must Honor Its Zoning Rules: A Dispute over Proposed Construction Raises the Specter of Changing Zoning Rules Based on Whims." *Denver Post*, 9 February 2012.
- "Neighbors Oppose Testo's Zone Change." *Connecticut Post*, 25 February 2012.
- "Some Neighbors Oppose 'Field of Dreams' Plan." *WCF Courier* (Iowa), 21 February 2012.
- "Neighbors Oppose Feedlot Expansion." *Norfolk Daily News*, 17 February 2012.

■ ■ ■

**View of the Public Garden and Boston Common (1829).**
Source: Boston Public Library.

Since colonial times, we have managed land use. The Puritans set aside the
Boston Common as a shared space to graze livestock. The descendants of the
Pilgrims protected the Province Lands on Cape Cod to ensure common access
to hunting and fishing. Many years later, the first, large skyscrapers were
built, and city dwellers confronted the new challenges of street congestion,
loss of light and air, overcrowding of land, and the need for public transportation. In the early 1900s, as America transitioned rapidly from a rural to an
urban society, city governments passed laws to gain greater control over land
development. In 1916, New York City was the first municipality in the United
States to address these challenges with a comprehensive approach to controlling development. Based on a model from Germany, the city council adopted
an ordinance that created zones designating appropriate uses. In 1926, the
U.S. Department of Commerce followed suit, developing a model "Standard
Zoning Enabling Act" based on New York City's ordinance. That same year, in
a case called *Village of Euclid v. Ambler Realty Co.*, 272 U.S. 365 (1926), the U.S.
Supreme Court determined that restricting the use of land through zoning
was permissible and did not violate the U.S. Constitution. All state legisla-

tures have since adopted similar models, creating a largely consistent, broad structure of land use control in this country (McQuillin 2011).

## THE INADEQUACY OF EXISTING PROCEDURES

Over the last one hundred years of land use management by local governments, a common approval process for decision making has developed. As shown in figure 1.2, there are essentially four stages. Applicants are required to file proposals with a local board or department. These plans are reviewed and sometimes modified and they often come before a planning board or zoning board of appeals. The applicant gives a presentation; the board asks questions, may request modifications, and hears public comment. The public body either makes a decision or forwards a recommendation to a final decision-making body such as a town or city council.

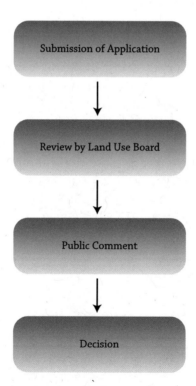

FIGURE 1.2 Land Use Approval: The Required Decision-Making Process

For controversial decisions, such as the Discordia example, the required process does not provide adequate opportunities for various groups with vested interests in the outcome to be heard or for the decision-making process to meet their needs. Neighbors testify in public comment periods, but are not given the opportunity to engage in a constructive dialogue. Developers have little incentive or ability to change proposals because the submission process requires expensive and elaborate plans from the start. Everyone withholds key information for fear the other side will somehow take advantage of them. Therefore, the public forum of the required process limits the opportunity for actual dialogue; instead it sets the stage for opposing claims, political positioning, and controversy.

Often people in conflict move to solve problems in court without actively exploring negotiation first. A study of mediation by the Vermont Environmental Court, which hears all land use appeals in that state, found that in roughly half of the cases studied the parties had never engaged in settlement negotiations before coming to court (Field, Strassberg, and Harvey 2009). This failure to talk has significant consequences. A study of intermunicipal mediation in Alberta, Canada, found that over three-quarters of the time and expense of a land use appeal is attributed to the final hearing and any appeals that challenge the decision (Alberta Municipal Affairs 2005). As the Alberta and Vermont reports show, the required process can result in a tremendous amount of wasted time and money when applied to controversial land use decisions.

This standard, required process works well for the majority of land use decisions. Most decisions made by land use boards using this process are made rather quickly and without much controversy. By a rough measure, a majority of a board's decisions are not controversial and only take up a small amount of its time. On the other hand, a minority of the decisions are controversial and can end up taking the majority of the board's time. When faced with controversial and complex decisions, communities often become embroiled in battles that tear at the civic fabric, pit neighbor against neighbor, demonize the applicant, and wear down local officials. Volunteer board members, neighbors, and applicants are often disheartened by what seems to be an insufficient process for solving these difficult, time consuming, heated land use disputes. The mutual gains approach presented in this book is appropriate for these controversial decisions.

## POWER AND RIGHTS CANNOT RESOLVE
## COMPLEX DISPUTES

When a community is faced with disputes on land use, the interactions
between stakeholders provide valuable lessons to help us understand
how disputes are managed. A decision-making system is "a coordinated
set of processes or mechanisms that interact with each other to prevent,
manage, and/or resolve disputes" (Bordone 2008, 2). The processes of land
use decision-making systems can vary in efficiency, effectiveness, and
satisfaction. According to the field of dispute system design, there are
three principal approaches to resolving disputes (Ury, Brett, and Goldberg
1988; Costantino and Sickles Merchant 1996).

- **Rely on power.** Use one's leverage to force or coerce someone to act.
- **Adjudicate rights.** Rely on an arbiter to decide who is right. Set up
  adjudicatory processes to determine who has legally enforceable rights
  and who does not.
- **Reconcile interests.** Try to satisfy needs, concerns, and fears of everyone involved.

These approaches help us analyze the limitations of the systems used
to resolve land use disputes. Most land use systems are designed to
adjudicate rights, not reconcile interests. Power- and rights-based
systems are less likely to produce durable outcomes because results can
be overturned when the power balance changes. In local communities,
the power balance is always shifting with new elections and court
challenges. While power and rights approaches may allow for quick
decisions, the results of those decisions are not likely to last or satisfy
many of the people involved, and they might be challenged through
administrative and judicial appeals. These approaches often destroy
relationships among the involved parties by creating winners and losers
and by fostering mistrust and hostility. Projects and decisions that
require long-term implementation depend on the support of a wide
range of stakeholders beyond the current elected officials to ensure their
sustainability over time. These are the decisions that are appropriate for
processes that reconcile interests.

The vast majority of land use decisions are easy to make. Does a landowner's request to build an addition fit within the zoning ordinance? Does the request for an area variance meet the requirements of the statute? Is the lighting proper? Is there enough off-street parking? From a systems perspective, most decisions are appropriately and efficiently handled by adjudicating rights. The standard, required process is a rights-based, adjudicatory process.

However, with some significant and complex decisions, parties have many interests that are not likely to be addressed in a rights-based approach. In addition, the questions raised in complicated decisions present many interconnected issues. These "polycentric" disputes make it difficult, if not impossible, for a board or a judge to find common ground. For example, can public access to a waterfront be enhanced while ensuring a successful, private development? Can new uses support or enhance adjacent, current land uses? Can new development contribute to the tax base for an entire community? These are questions that are better answered by the most-affected stakeholders through interest-based processes. If the board assumes the rights-based process is appropriate in more complex decisions, it will likely miss an opportunity to reconcile numerous, important community interests.

Communities have a choice when it comes to process: they can continue using the rights-based, required process for all types of decisions, which may deter people from participating, create deep divides among segments of the community, and overlook opportunities for creative problem solving; or they can use a different process appropriate for the nature of the decision being made.

Many communities decide to supplement regular processes with the mutual gains approach. These communities have learned that people may shift perspectives when allowed to learn jointly and explore interests, generate options from those interests, and build trust in the process and in each other. Some communities have enacted provisions that require preapplication meetings between the developer and potentially affected citizens (Gardiner 2008). Some developers have convened ad hoc advisory committees to help craft appropriate plans for the community prior to submitting an application (Nolon 2009). Some local officials have encouraged disputants to put the decision-making process on hold while they enlist the help of a mediator to see if agreement can be reached in a different forum (*Merson v. McNally*, 90 N.Y.2d 742 [1997]). Many courts across the country have instituted mediation programs to encourage and support parties in reaching agreement prior to court in an effort to prevent costly, lengthy, and unpredictable court proceedings. This book examines the common features of these processes and provides a framework to apply them in your community.

## A PREFERRED WAY TO MANAGE CONTENTIOUS SITUATIONS

In over a decade of research sponsored by the Lincoln Institute of Land Policy and with years of professional experience, we have found there is a better way to manage the most challenging situations. The mutual gains approach is not a single process or technique. It draws from the fields of negotiation, consensus building, collaborative problem solving, alternative dispute resolution, public participation, public administration, and deliberative democracy. The mutual gains approach is different from the required land use processes in its goals, intended audience, structure, methods, and decision making.

### Mutual Gains Approach Versus the Required Process

The mutual gains approach is guided by core principles, follows a set of clear action steps, and is useful at various stages of land use decision making. It is different from, though not incompatible with, the required land use procedures. Appropriate in those cases where an impasse has arisen or is likely to arise, the mutual gains approach

- is based on all stakeholder interests as well as the necessary technical information;
- involves stakeholders along with appointed and elected decision makers;
- generates information relevant and salient to stakeholders, including abutters, community leaders, and others;
- requires strong community and public engagement skills along with strong, technical planning skills; and
- engages the public above and beyond sharing information and views.

The mutual gains approach is not limited to any one phase of the land use decision-making process. It may be used early on to help prepare a municipality-wide, comprehensive or master plan prior to an application being filed, prior to or during the public hearing process, or even after a decision has been made.

In planning efforts, communities can use charrettes (a kind of public design studio), public workshops, stakeholder committees, and other tools to build greater understanding and consensus around neighborhood or community-wide plans. Even before an application is filed for a particular project, a proponent can meet with potentially affected stakeholders to share ideas and learn about people's concerns and issues in order to build a better plan going forward. Once an application or proposed plan is submitted, municipal officials, citizens, and project proponents have at their disposal a range of process options.

The mutual gains approach, as compared to the required procedures, is summarized in table 1.1.

The mutual gains approach incorporates two key dimensions: (1) the *principles* that inform the approach; and (2) the *steps* of this approach. While the stories in this book are often complex, involving long disputes

TABLE 1.1
**The Required Versus the Mutual Gains Approach**

|  | *Required* | *Mutual Gains* |
|---|---|---|
| **Goal** | A technically viable plan that conforms to all laws, rules, and regulations | A technically viable plan that integrates stakeholder interests |
| **Primary Audience for Plan or Project** | Decision makers | Decision makers and stakeholders |
| **Purpose of Data and Information** | To ensure the plan conforms to professional practice and passes technical review | To ensure the plan is feasible and addresses stakeholders' issues and concerns |
| **Skills** | Technical (engineering, design, and fiscal) and legal | Technical, legal, and community engagement (dialogue and deliberation) |
| **Role of Public** | Provide input and advice | Engage in discussion, joint problem solving, and consensus building |

and stakeholder engagement processes, the principles and steps described may be used in situations as simple as a single meeting. This approach, tailored to fit, can work on multiple scales.

## Principles of the Mutual Gains Approach to Managing Politics and Process

A review of hundreds of cases makes clear that the most successful mutual gains processes incorporate the same key principles. While every situation and context require flexibility, the most effective processes incorporate the following:

- Engage early.
- Listen and learn first.
- Build on interests, not positions.
- Design and build an effective process.
- Involve many, not just a few.
- Learn jointly.
- Use a skilled facilitator.
- Build relationships for the long term.

Throughout this book, these principles are used in both real and hypothetical cases. When these principles are followed, they can result in productive engagement rather than adversarial forms of interaction with the public. The principles should be woven through each of the four steps of the collaborative mutual gains process: assessment, design, deliberation, and implementation.

- ***Engage Early.*** Leaders, decision makers, and key parties should begin collaborating with stakeholders as early as possible in the development process. Early on, people are less likely to be committed to a particular vision or outcome, and design and engineering work are still preliminary. In the early stages there is more opportunity to change the proposal and to respond to feedback and ideas from key groups. Engaging early provides those involved the luxury of time to work through differences and increase trust and transparency. This will also allow the parties to identify the full range of concerns early on and to address those interests in the proposal. This is in stark contrast to what typically happens when stakeholder interests are discovered later, when it is less practical to alter a proposal due to time and budgetary constraints.

- **Listen and Learn First.** The best tools for reaching a workable solution to a complicated situation are listening and understanding. Thus, we recommend an assessment process (formal or informal, small or large) to identify key stakeholders, learn about their interests and concerns, and hear how they want to be involved. It is impossible to effectively address concerns about a proposed development without understanding the hopes and fears behind those concerns.

- **Build on Interests, Not Positions.** Through over 40 years of research on negotiation, we know that parties have the best chance of success if they understand from the start what their counterparts care about and why. Rather than simply stating their positions, which are often in opposition to one another, parties should focus on their interests. Positions are the outcomes people believe will satisfy their underlying interests. Interests explain why people care about an issue, what motivates them, and what they deem important. This distinction may be characterized in this way:

> POSITION: *What I want or demand. For example, I do not want more than 50 parking spaces in the lot near my home.*

> INTEREST: *Why I want what I want, or the underlying reasons for my stated position. For example, I am very concerned about traffic congestion and not being able to get through the intersection quickly on my way home.*

Processes that help parties tease out interests, invent options based on those interests, and find ways to select options that meet the shared interests are most likely to result in stable, wise, and fair outcomes. If well identified, interests can serve as the building blocks for options and approaches to satisfy the parties. For example, one may respond to the above position by asking, "If you are worried about heavy traffic; can we explore ways to ensure that traffic will be controlled in the new development?" Too often, the conventional, "offer and counteroffer" dynamic does not create innovative options that address multiple interests.

- *Design and Build an Effective Process.* Each community and conflict has a unique context and set of dynamics. It is important to design a process tailored to the specific situation, structured around the interests and concerns of the stakeholders. The design must be coordinated with the formal, decision-making authority and existing administrative procedures (as required for any project to be legitimate and legally defensible).

- *Involve Many, Not Just a Few.* Engage those with a broad range of perspectives who may be affected (both positively and negatively), rather than merely working with the customary community leaders, planners, elected officials, power brokers, and those few who have legal standing in the final appeal. You are more likely to reduce opposition and make new allies if you engage more than the few people in positions of power.

- *Learn Jointly.* Land use planning and development is a complex process with multiple economic, environmental, and social impacts. Because the development community is sometimes seen as suspect in the eyes of the public, it is important to present technical information that is accurate, factual, and trusted. Likewise, neighborhood or environmental groups may be mistrusted as they enter into a conflict. These community groups deserve the opportunity to share their local knowledge and to be included in the discussion. For example, reviewing traffic studies that are completed by a jointly selected consultant, sharing the data, bringing in experts on design and development, and planning activities together will increase the level of trust in the information available and, ultimately, in the process itself.

- *Use a Skilled Facilitator.* Given the number of stakeholders and the complexity of issues and influencing factors, it is difficult to successfully manage deliberation and joint problem solving. Position taking, adverse reactions, disagreement, and misinformation may result. Thus, actively facilitating and coordinating the process will improve outcomes of multistakeholder processes. This may be accomplished through technical tools, independent facilitators, or skilled internal staff.

- *Build Relationships for the Long Term.* The very nature of land use decisions involves the construction or alteration of physical space. The people and organizations involved will live with these decisions for years. Given the long-term nature of development, it is essential that parties work to build and maintain good relationships. One way to do this is to make decisions transparent and consistent. Effective processes seek to inform and include stakeholders early and often, share information to the greatest extent possible, provide parties advance notice of proposals, changes, and information, and ensure that the process is clear and open. Reducing the element of surprise can build the community's trust that citizens will be informed and that they will have a chance to weigh in meaningfully.

### Steps to Implement a Mutual Gains Approach

In addition to the underlying principles, there are four general steps in implementing a mutual gains process. These four activities are discussed in more detail in chapters 4–7.

- *Assess and Understand Stakeholders, Issues, and Interests.* In order to bring people together, a small group needs to determine who should be involved, what topics should be addressed, and how the process should be structured. This is called an *assessment*. Assessment is the broad task of gathering information about stakeholders and their perspectives, which is a key step in understanding the situation thoroughly enough to make well-informed decisions about how to proceed. This evaluation is a series of confidential interviews with key stakeholders, often carried out by an impartial professional (such as a mediator or facilitator), that results in summary findings and recommendations. Assessment results identify critical issues, help determine who needs to be involved in the process, and aid in developing a plan of action.

    Assessments can be as simple as talking to 10 people from a variety of stakeholder groups and giving an oral presentation at a public meeting of what was learned, or as complex as interviewing 100 people over many months and preparing a lengthy report detailing a complex history and opportunities for moving forward. The type of assessment used depends on the nature of the conflict and available resources. (See chapter 4.)

- *Design a Process for Collaboration.* Process design is the deliberate effort to identify the key elements and conditions that must be put in place to enable people to work together well. Good process design serves the community just as good infrastructure does. You cannot build a thriving city without the necessary infrastructure (water, streets, sewer, and open space) and you are not likely to create durable, widely supported decisions without sufficient process structure. Good process design can channel conflict productively, ensure meaningful stakeholder engagement, define both problems and solutions, identify what people care about most, generate creative and nuanced options, and increase the likelihood of broad agreement among stakeholders. (See chapter 5 for examples and characteristics of good process design.)

■ *Facilitate Deliberation.* A mutual gains approach always involves some form of deliberation in which people work together. This may take the form of face-to-face meetings or may deploy any number of technological solutions from keypad polling to online visioning tools. There are three broad phases of deliberation: *the beginning*, when groups form and establish some kind of norms, scope, and focus; *the middle*, when groups identify their interests, gather technical information, manage their relationships with one another, and generate options to create added value; and *the end*, when groups narrow choices, package components of a solution, and strive to reach agreement (see figure 1.3).

Processes that address a limited number of issues may tackle all three phases in one or two meetings, as often occurs in the mediation of simpler cases. Other processes may take one or more years and multiple phases. Though these phases of deliberation may seem linear and simple, this three-phase framework provides a useful structure to prepare for the challenges that may arise during deliberation. (See chapter 6 for more on deliberation.)

■ *Implement Agreements.* In the same way that assessment and process design are often ignored or rushed, the implementation of outcomes is often given inadequate attention. After working hard to reach an agreement, stakeholders (most of whom are volunteers) are eager to return to their lives. They feel that their job was to reach an agreement and, once that is accomplished, their work is done. Reaching agreement, however, is not necessarily the end of a collaborative process.

| I. Beginning | | II. Middle | | III. End |
|---|---|---|---|---|
| The group clarifies how it will work together by: | → | The group identifies interests, gathers information, and generates options by: | → | The group narrows choices, develops an implementation plan, and reaches agreement by: |

I. Beginning

The group clarifies how it will work together by:

- Establishing norms
- Guaranteeing confidentiality
- Developing decision rules
- Creating appropriate agendas
- Managing logistics
- Engaging key participants and the media

II. Middle

The group identifies interests, gathers information, and generates options by:

- Surfacing interests
- Building trust
- Dealing with difficult people
- Generating ideas
- Developing a work plan
- Managing first offers

III. End

The group narrows choices, develops an implementation plan, and reaches agreement by:

- Using deadlines
- Breaking through impasses
- Generating packages
- Drafting agreements

FIGURE 1.3 Three Phases of Deliberation

During deliberation, the parties will have identified a solution that satisfies as many needs and interests as possible. Once that agreement is reached, the outcomes must become legally enforceable or required in ordinances or other formal agreements; stakeholders must stay involved to ensure that their hard work is realized. Constantly changing conditions at the local level necessitate planning for implementation. Staff turnover, changing political players, and unstable market conditions should be anticipated in most land use decisions. Conveners and stakeholders must plan for such surprises.

In the implementation stage, three tasks must be completed. First, the recommendations are incorporated into a proposal for a plan, an ordinance, or a development. This proposal must meet the requirements of the decision-making board while incorporating the recommendations from the agreement. Second, the application is reviewed by the decision-making board and is subject to the standard decision-making process. Parties to the agreement must advise the board of their work and recommendations during the review process. Third, if approved, the plan must be implemented, the ordinance administered, or the development built. (See chapter 7 for more on implementation.)

## Key Negotiation Concepts

While this book does not focus on negotiation theory, several negotiation concepts are essential in the mutual gains approach and warrant review. (See Fisher, Ury, and Patton 1991, for more explanation.)

- *Explore Interests, Not Merely Positions.* As previously discussed, positions are assertions about what someone wants or demands: "I want no changes to the local strip mall next to me." Interests refer to the "why" of someone's position, one's underlying needs, desires, and concerns: "I want no changes because I shop at the local grocery store in the mall every day, am afraid of construction disruption to my neighborhood, and feel new development will be too big and bring too much traffic." It is important to explore underlying interests early because (1) there may be multiple ways to satisfy interests beyond the stated position; (2) early statements of position tend to increase oppositional behavior; and (3) different approaches may be precluded because the position has already been stated, making it difficult to back down.

- *Determine Best Alternatives to a Negotiated Agreement (BATNAs).* Negotiation theory and practice have shown that the areas of possible agreement or the bargaining range for a negotiation are powerfully shaped by what the parties believe they could do on their own if there were no negotiation. If they do not talk through the issue together, what other actions might they take (political, legal, personal, or financial)? If there is no discussion or negotiation, citizens may instead write letters to the editor or make bumper stickers to express their views; environmental groups might organize a campaign or litigate; or a developer might seek to prevail in court. BATNAs shape the scope and possibility at the bargaining table. If one party believes they can get a vote passed at city council, for instance, it may be less willing to make compromises with neighbors or other stakeholders. On the other hand, if citizens determine that they have a weak best alternative, they may decide to increase their power by building alliances, reaching out to the press, or other means. All stakeholders have alternatives to negotiating.

- *Create Value.* It is frequently assumed that negotiation only involves allocating pieces of a fixed pie among stakeholders. Negotiation is thought to merely determine who gets what: Who are the winners and losers? But effective negotiations expand the pie for all parties. Participants can expand the pie by coming up with new solutions together that meet their multiple interests through processes such as brainstorming. When participants propose solutions that meet many interests, they are effectively enlarging the pie. Time and time again, we have seen people work together in a structured process and create ideas that are better than any previously discussed and that everyone can support. This is one of the benefits of the supplemental mutual gains approach that is often missing from the conventional, required decision-making process.

- **Base Decisions on Joint Criteria.** The required processes of land use decision making rely on criteria or rules established through state laws, local ordinances, and other regulations and policies. But often these criteria are not sufficient to address most or all of the underlying interests of the multiple parties. A setback, for instance, might be 100 feet from a wetland. But a developer may make the case to the town and environmental advocates that spending more money on additional, natural, storm water management (swales and variable vegetated buffers around the development) can produce a better environmental outcome than merely adhering to a specific setback.

  The criteria of cost, appearance, and preservation of open space might be used to select among several designs the architect has developed. Open space organizations may care most about the environment while neighbors might be more interested in the style of the design. Furthermore, in the required process that involves only a few public officials and developers, other stakeholders may have the sense that backroom deals are being made if they do not know the criteria used in arriving at a final decision. A more public, collaborative process can tease out the range of interests and criteria, compare various alternatives, and determine which alternatives satisfy the most interests.

## Case Studies

This book features case studies from across the United States and Canada, summarized in table 1.2, to illustrate the principles and steps in the mutual gains process.

**TABLE 1.2**

**Cases: Various Outcomes of the Mutual Gains Approach**

| Case Name/Location | Year | Description | Outcome |
|---|---|---|---|
| Assembly Square/ Somerville, Massachusetts | 1998–2007, and ongoing | For nearly a decade, disagreements impeded creation of redevelopment plans for Assembly Square, a former economic and manufacturing hub declared a blighted district by the City of Somerville. | Disputing parties negotiated an agreement in 2006 that addressed the short- and long-term land plans. Litigation was dropped and agreements were reached to continue to fund public transportation, study health effects, create green space, and establish an employment-training program. Development began in 2012. |
| Borderland Village Innovation Pilot/ Killingly, Connecticut | 2008–2010 | Guided by technical experts, residents participated in planning exercises to preserve a critical habitat and the rural character of the community by integrating new development into town centers and clustering development to preserve one of the last wildlife corridors on the East Coast. | The collaborative processes resulted in final reports that provided recommendations for inclusive research and implementation processes for future planning efforts. |
| Chelsea Salt Dock/ Chelsea, Massachusetts | 2002–2003 | Long-term conflicts among municipal, residential, and industrial users led to a mediation to discuss mitigation and resiting of the salt dock. | The mediation did not result in a final settlement, but it led to restoration of relationships among the parties and additional mitigation measures. |
| Downtown Planning Process/Meriden, Connecticut | 2004–2005 | The City Center Advisory Group, which represented 20 stakeholder groups, was formed to address issues associated with the City of Meriden's downtown redevelopment plans. | The process produced a report detailing the four main obstacles to redevelopment and how to overcome them. |
| Hercules, California | 2000 | Historically, development in Hercules was poorly planned. To remedy this, the Hercules Planning Commission used a 10-day charrette to gather citizen input and plan the development of a town center *before* developer proposals were accepted. | The charrette enabled community members and elected officials to avoid conflict and collaboratively plan a walkable, mixed-use neighborhood with the first form-based code in California. |

TABLE 1.2 (continued)

| Case Name/Location | Year | Description | Outcome |
| --- | --- | --- | --- |
| Homeless Shelter/ West Chester, Pennsylvania | 1994–1995 | Growing signs of socioeconomic stress in the city of West Chester led local charitable foundations to form a nonprofit shelter, Safe Harbor of Greater West Chester. The shelter was to provide meals and counseling for the homeless. However, the proposed location for the shelter, near the city's downtown business district, raised concern and ire from nearby businesses and neighbors. | The shelter was eventually approved after the applicant made assurances that addressed concerns of neighbors. |
| J. P. Carrara Mine/ East Middlebury, Vermont | 2007–2009 | The J. P. Carrara gravel company applied for a permit to expand a mine onto adjacent land. Community members, upset with the expansion, formed a group to discuss the issues. Eventually the developer joined the group. | The collaborative process produced an amended permit application that included mitigation measures proposed by the parties. |
| Leonard P. Zakim Bunker Hill Memorial Bridge/Boston, Massachusetts | 1990–1992 | Disagreements over the design of the Charles River Crossing brought lawsuits that threatened progress on the Central Artery/Tunnel project. | A committee of 42 members drafted a bridge design proposal that the State of Massachusetts eventually adopted. |
| MaxPak/Somerville, Massachusetts | 2004–2005 | Residents raised concerns about excessive noise, air pollution, traffic congestion, and soil contamination in a city plan to densely redevelop a former industrial brownfield site. The city required the developer to solicit community input through an engagement process, which the city ultimately facilitated. | The community planning process resulted in a concerns-and-recommendations report that offered guidelines for site development. After a yearlong planning effort, a preliminary master plan for a 199-unit, residential development surrounded by green space was approved in 2008. |

| Project/Location | Year | Description | Outcome |
|---|---|---|---|
| Mill Plaza/Durham, New Hampshire | 2006–2008 | The Mill Plaza Study Committee, formed as part of a private developer's community engagement plan, created a conceptual design for a central, downtown property that the public would support and the city would permit. | The committee produced seven recommendations to create a pedestrian-friendly downtown that incorporated green building standards and carbon-neutral principles that conserved an important waterway. |
| North 4th Street Corridor/Albuquerque, New Mexico | 2007–2008 | Residents and merchants disagreed with the City of Albuquerque's draft redevelopment plan and the process used to create it. Representatives of the stakeholders used overlay zoning plans, satellite imagery, and interest-based discussions to create a set of development recommendations. | The representative stakeholder group drafted its recommendations and presented them to the Environmental Planning Commission (EPC). The City of Albuquerque redrafted the plan and gained the support of residents and merchants. The EPC approved the plan in 2009. |
| Streamlining Community Planning/Falmouth, Maine | 2007 | The Town of Falmouth sought to engage the community in a facilitated dialogue to reach a shared vision and plan for improving the effectiveness and efficiency of its complex community development and planning system. | With the help of mediators, town decision makers reached a shared vision and a realistic plan for revising and implementing short- and long-term improvements to the town's land use and community development systems. |
| Threshold Process/ San Mateo County, California | 2008 | An affordable housing shortage in San Mateo compelled Threshold 2008 to engage community members in discussion about housing issues and options to ensure an improved, long-term quality of life for those affected by housing choices. | The process helped housing advocates, policy makers, and other participants of Threshold 2008 understand the issues more clearly. The project continued as Threshold 2009 to increase civic engagement in government practice. |
| Wind Turbine Farm/ Manchester, Vermont | 2005–2006 | The Orton Family Foundation began a community engagement process to clarify citizens' interests and concerns about a proposed, five-turbine wind farm. | In a town board meeting following these discussions, the community narrowly voted to allocate funds to oppose the project. |

# CHAPTER 2

■ ■ □ □ □ □ □ □ □

# Safety, Profit, and Due Process: The History and Purpose of Land Use Decisions

Three major goals of the government's land use decision-making system are (1) to protect health, safety, and welfare of citizens; (2) to allow for individual and community benefit; and (3) to protect the due process rights of property owners and citizens. This chapter explores the system of land development in the United States by describing the decision-making process local governments are required to use and how the mutual gains approach can be integrated into that process. Very often officials, accustomed to the required process, do not view other decision-making options favorably. Yet, in reality, the required decision-making process provides ample opportunity to integrate a mutual gains process before, during, and after a decision.

We develop land to provide places to live, work, worship, congregate, shop, and recreate. We have altered the natural landscape, creating an environment of buildings, walls, windows, parks, and roads. Although citizens have a range of feelings about construction and development, there is no denying their importance to human existence. Development of land allows for activities that enhance and ensure our survival and it can inspire us. Egyptian and Mayan pyramids, the Parthenon, and the Taj Mahal are examples of developments that connect to an essential part of our humanity. The way we interact with developed spaces affects our experience and enjoyment—an afternoon game at Wrigley Field, jazz at the Hollywood Bowl, chamber music at Avery Fisher Hall, or a stroll along a country lane.

Development also serves important economic purposes, bringing new life to cities and towns through the introduction of new shops, restaurants, and businesses. This type of development can increase the local tax base, create new jobs and educational opportunities, and provide other essential benefits to communities, such as infrastructure for water, sewers, roads, and telecommunications facilities.

However, development can also create significant problems. Shoddy construction, poorly located buildings, and incompatible uses in close proximity can cause serious harm, injury, and even death. When development fouls the air, pollutes the waters, and contaminates the soil, we all suffer. When monotonous, repetitive, and out-of-scale development dominates our landscape, we lose interest and a sense of investment in our community, our fellow humans, and ourselves (Brown 2009; Hess 2009). Poorly designed development significantly detracts from the enjoyment of our spaces and our sense of community. For these reasons, development without proper precautions can cause more harm than benefit.

We rely on local government to balance these functions of protection and benefit, creating tension in our relationship with the government. We count on government to boost the local economy and promote business, but we do not want our community to be negatively impacted by such development. We want the government to protect individual citizens while also protecting the collective community. We want to be safe, but we do not want to be told what to do. The perception of governmental action as simultaneously positive and negative is shaped by both the *substantive* provisions of a law (what behaviors or actions are allowed or prohibited) and the *procedural* components of the law (processes used to adopt and implement the law). People may object to the substance of a law that restricts development and may also object to the procedures used to create and pass the law. In other situations, people may not be offended by the substance but may care about the process used to pass the law. Citizens may object to the treatment of people, the lack of inclusivity, or the limited information provided to the public during the decision-making process.

## THE PURPOSE OF THE REQUIRED PROCESS

In order to make valid, defensible land use decisions, government must follow the procedures and practices required by law. At the core of these practices are two purposes: to protect legally recognized rights and to provide the required notice of an impending decision. The government is responsible for protecting the rights of all parties (individuals, communities, and developers) and also for communicating to these stakeholders. A local law may require an applicant to give adjacent property owners 30 days' notice before a hearing. If that law is not followed, a decision may be challenged and overturned.

## THE CONSEQUENCES OF THE
## REQUIRED PROCESS

While the required land use decision-making process is sufficient for routine cases, it can encourage adversarial interactions among decision makers, applicants, and the community when used in controversial development projects. It does not foster communication between the landowner and interested citizens because interactions are directed to the government arbiter and exchanged in a trial-like environment. As a result, the applicant and community are often placed in opposition to one another, clearly discouraging communication and productive relationships.

After the developer submits a proposal and the process formally begins, most required processes do not provide the community with an official opportunity to comment on the project for weeks, if not months. The level of citizen participation required by law is limited to commentary at a hearing or a written response to the submitted application. The format of the process (proponents and opponents providing written and oral arguments to a single arbiter) signals from the start that conflict is expected. As a result, the stakeholders perceive each other as adversaries who are competing for the governmental decision. In routine land development matters, this adversarial dynamic may not become a problem. In controversial, complex development decisions, however, it presents a considerable obstacle to reaching satisfying outcomes.

## THE LIMITATIONS OF THE
## REQUIRED PROCESS

The required process easily addresses decisions that involve few parties and present fairly simple issues. This includes proposals for small subdivisions and simple site plan applications. In these situations the landowner submits an application, it is reviewed, concerned parties provide comments, and the government makes a decision in a timely manner. When a party's interests are consistent with the rights codified in existing law, the required process will likely produce a satisfying outcome.

Most land use decisions made by the local boards fall into this category and are handled in a timely manner. More complex and controversial land use decisions are fewer in number but take more time to resolve. When parties rely only on the required process to resolve significant land development disputes, the normally efficient process can devolve into an unpredictable, expensive, and frustrating experience.

For example, highly contentious decisions often intensify the approval process. It is not unusual for people to wear buttons, carry signs, and applaud at public hearings to bring attention to their cause. The applicants may present a parade of experts and advisors to advance their ideas. Board members may engage in elaborate efforts to appear neutral despite pressures to reveal their biases. Parties become consumed with trying to win the battle instead of working constructively to identify appropriate solutions. Their interactions can become fueled by misinformation and fear. Significant resources may be spent to advance their position by spinning facts, undermining the other party, and fighting over procedural missteps, instead of seeking constructive ways to resolve the dispute. Applicants can engage in competitive behaviors that encourage deception, manipulation, and even corruption. Neighbors may challenge the applicant and attempt to intimidate the government with threats of political retribution. Government representatives may feel forced to focus on surviving in elected office and making defensible decisions rather than on achieving a mutually beneficial solution. Decisions involving controversial issues often require innovative solutions and processes that encourage creativity instead of stifling it.

## THE ROLES OF THE STAKEHOLDERS IN THE REQUIRED PROCESS

Land use decisions involve multiple parties. While each decision is different, some consistent roles are played in each process. Three roles are explored here: the government, the landowner, and the community.

## The Role of the Government

The government serves as both the accelerator and the brake for the development of land. It creates plans and adopts laws that allow for the development of land and are its principal tools in controlling that development. For example, local laws can streamline approvals for development applications that meet certain conditions or, conversely, impose conditions that make moving forward much more difficult. The government's role is to create the framework that identifies where development should be allowed and where it should not, to establish appropriate decision-making processes, and to make decisions consistent with its enabling legislation.

## The Role of the Landowner

Landowners play both a private and a public role when developing land. First and foremost, the project must provide some form of benefit to the owner. Second, however, the project must advance the goals of the community as stated in the zoning ordinance and comprehensive plan. If a proposed project does not comply with the governing laws, it should be denied.

## The Role of the Community

The community's role in land development is to provide input, elect representatives, and ensure maximization of benefit. Citizens are often the end users of the development (e.g., a local park, a downtown area, or transportation improvements) and will have to live with any negative impacts, so they should monitor development proposals. In a sense, the community sits as a jury, judging the actions of the government and the landowner. If the government does not pay sufficient attention to adverse impacts or does not follow the proper process, the community has the power to oppose, adjust, delay, or stop decisions. In addition, the community has indirect and informal authority to influence the decision-making process through comments at public meetings, boycotts, media campaigns, elections, and referenda.

In many decisions, especially controversial ones, the community will speak with many voices. Managing this diversity of opinion is often a principal objective when designing a process. Planners have spent the last several decades promoting the importance of consensus-building techniques to gather and integrate the diversity of opinion in such cases (Tomain 1989). Planners are in a unique position to determine which members of the public should be engaged, how to contact them, and how best to collect their input.

## THE CONTEXT OF DISCORDIA

The project proposed for the hypothetical, mid-sized municipality of Discordia sheds light on the typical decision-making process. As outlined in chapter 1, the three-acre parcel with the dilapidated mall fronts on to a four-lane road, is across the street from a supermarket, is flanked by a bank and a small office building, and backs onto a school in a residential neighborhood.

In the 1950s, elected officials in Discordia passed a local law that divided the community into separate zones and permitted specific uses (such as residential, commercial, and industrial) in different zones. The law also required the formation of a planning board to hear applications and a zoning board of appeals to hear challenges to the law. According to the law, commercial and office uses are allowed in the zone where the Discordia mall is located.

The new owners of the mall propose to demolish the existing one-story building and build in its place two three-story buildings with commercial space on the ground floor and two floors of offices above. They feel that their proposed building fits the historical and architectural style of Discordia and will better serve the changing needs of the community while meeting market demands. Based on local laws, changing the footprint of the building, adding more floors, and introducing a new use—offices—trigger the need for a "conditional use permit" from the planning board.

Conditional use permits are designed to ensure that specific uses will not conflict with the other uses allowed in that zone. For example, many residential zones allow uses such as nursery schools, subject to conditions that ensure compatibility with the predominant residential uses. In addition to satisfying the requirements of the conditional use permits, most developments must also comply with site plan approval. The board reviews the location of the building; the materials proposed; the infrastructure such as electric, sewer, and water lines; the layout of parking spaces; landscaping; lighting; storm water management; and the traffic flow.

Once the application is submitted, ordinances require the applicant to give notice to the property owners near the parcel before a public hearing can be held. In Discordia, applicants for a conditional use permit must give 45 days' notice to all property owners within 500 feet of the parcel. There are six such properties including the National Bank, the Petroil gas station, the Super-Mart, the Burns Medical Complex, Quimby Elementary School, and a garden apartment complex called Bailey Apartments. With the stage set in Discordia, the remainder of this chapter explores how the land use decision-making process will decide the future of this parcel.

## THE EFFECTS OF ZONING

The history of land use law gives insight into how Discordia might deal with this land use decision. The *Euclid* case referenced in chapter 1 is a good example of how municipalities have used zoning to regulate the development of land. In that case, Ambler Realty owned 68 acres of land in the village of Euclid, a suburb of Cleveland, Ohio. The village, in an effort to limit urban growth from Cleveland, adopted an ordinance that created six classes of uses and identified appropriate zones for those uses. Ambler's 68 acres fell into three separate zones. Ambler Realty sued the village, claiming that the new law illegally took away its property rights to develop the entire parcel at the highest density. The Court found that the zoning ordinance was constitutional because it was enacted to benefit the entire community and that the law was adequately crafted to accomplish that benefit.

The rationale for adopting zoning ordinances is to protect the public from the harmful effects of development. The authority to adopt zoning ordinances originates in the states' inherent authority to protect health, safety, and welfare. This authority, generally referred to as the "police power," allows government to protect the public from a variety of actions including "private acts considered to be unreasonable to society" (Platt 2004, 292). The use of land in a manner that harms others by causing excessive erosion or noise is an example of an act that can be regulated under the police power. In drafting our federal Constitution, the states did not delegate the police power to the federal government but instead retained it for their use. Today, through a variety of authorities, each state has delegated the land use regulation portion of its police power to county and local governments.

Much has changed since 1916 when New York City implemented the first zoning law. The pace and scale of land development in the United States has moved toward lower-density urbanization. In 1790, approximately 95 percent of Americans lived in rural areas (of which the United States had vast amounts). According to the 2010 Census, 80 percent of Americans lived in large metropolitan areas (urban and suburban areas). The last 50 years have seen the rapid growth of suburbs and the urbanization of the South and Southwest. The city of Las Vegas has increased from a sleepy population of 19 in 1900 to a bustling 580,000 in 2010. The Dallas–Fort Worth, Houston, and Atlanta metropolitan areas added more than 1,000,000 residents between 2000 and 2010 (U.S. Census data). Advances in engineering, architecture, and finance have allowed development in ways that were unimaginable in 1916. As a result, land use regulation has become increasingly complex. For example, New York City's first zoning ordinance was 44 pages long; today the code numbers over 3,000 pages and fills 13 separate volumes with multiple chapters in each volume.

Over the years, zoning laws have been adapted to address new development challenges. In the early 1900s, the principal issues were overcrowding, traffic, shadows from buildings, and flow of air in urban settings. In the 1940s and 1950s, zoning was used to regulate the development of suburban areas to deal with increased demand for housing. In the 1970s and 1980s, zoning techniques were developed to protect local environmental resources from being degraded by sprawling residential and commercial development. Recently, zoning has been used to encourage sustainable development and require green building techniques. The consistent vein running through all zoning and land use law is the goal of protecting public health, safety, and welfare.

However, local governments have frequently failed to deliver on their obligation to protect communities from harm and uphold their due process obligations. Many poor but functional neighborhoods have been destroyed in the name of urban redevelopment and progress. The Cross Bronx Expressway slashed the Tremont neighborhood into two sections; neighborhoods around the Loop in Chicago were razed and residents (mostly African-American) were forced into high-rise projects such as

Cabrini Green. In San Francisco, the vibrant and diverse Fillmore district was destroyed by the urban renewal policies of the 1950s. Similarly, many municipalities have used zoning to create homogeneous, segregated communities resulting in high prices and de facto exclusion of low-income families. Some municipalities have used zoning ordinances to ban multi-family housing as a way to exclude lower-income residents. The level of exclusion has reached such disturbing proportions that federal and state governments have imposed limits on local zoning authority. In New York and New Jersey, the courts responded to exclusionary zoning practices by limiting the ability of local governments to zone out multifamily housing (Nolon 1986).

The intentional misuse of zoning by some communities has generated significant local and national backlashes. The 1970s Sagebrush Rebellion in the West, the 1980s and 1990s Wise-Use Movement, and the more recent anti–eminent domain backlash spurred by the Supreme Court's decision in *Kelo v. City of New London*, 545 U.S. 469 (2005), are examples of regional and national efforts to limit local, land use authority. Many political campaigns have been started in response to dissatisfaction with how land use decisions have been handled. A signage law may forbid roadside farm stands from advertising. Variance procedures may delay otherwise simple decisions on technicalities. Boards may work to delay making a decision until the applicant gives up. Frustration in the community can lead to confrontation and political upheaval. In an extreme example, in 2004 a citizen, angered by a zoning dispute, ran his bulldozer through the town hall and other buildings of Granby, Colorado, causing millions of dollars in damages.

In response to perceived abuses of power at the local level, federal and state governments have passed laws limiting local, land use authority in several areas. For example, the federal Telecommunications Act (1996) makes it illegal for local governments to prohibit cellular phone towers on the basis that they adversely impact health. Similarly, the Religious Land Use and Institutionalized Persons Act (2000) prohibits local governments from imposing substantial burdens on religious exercise. There are many other examples, such as wetland protection, restrictions on land uses near schools, and restrictions on locations of group homes and homeless shelters, in which federal and state laws have been passed to limit the power of local zoning.

## HOW SAFETY, PROFIT, AND DUE PROCESS
## SHAPE LAND USE DECISION MAKING

The process and location of development depends on what is legally and politically permissible and whether financing is available. Most development projects must conform to the law and market demands (to obtain necessary financing), which makes land development a public and private endeavor. In most situations, to be successful, a development project must be safe and produce some profit or community benefit, and the approval process must satisfy due process.

### Development Must Be Safe

Development must provide some human benefit. Housing, hospitals, offices, airports, museums, and stores are all built to meet human needs, such as shelter, medical care, congregation, and commerce. Despite the benefits, the construction processes can cause extensive damage to a wide range of community and natural resources. Construction can change the flow of water across the land, increase impervious surfaces, destroy habitat, or degrade existing infrastructure such as roads, sewers, and utilities. In addition, the actual developments have the potential to harm human health—factories emit pollutants, traffic endangers pedestrians, and poorly built structures can cause physical injury through fire and collapse. Pollution cuts across local, state, and national borders. Fire can sweep from one home to another or even from one jurisdiction to another. Using groundwater for municipal drinking water can affect agricultural users outside city limits.

Most industrialized nations, including the United States, safeguard human health by passing protective laws and ordinances. Regulation of development is nothing new—society has controlled the development of land for thousands of years. As early as 400 B.C.E., the Chinese imposed land use controls to protect the public from river flooding. The Romans required buildings to be set back from property lines to allow for the flow of air, light, and water. In the United States we have extensive land use controls that limit how land is developed. The rationale behind most of these controls is to minimize both direct and indirect threats to human health associated with the development and use of land. Fire, disease, and flooding are examples of direct threats, while loss of habitat, groundwater depletion, and air pollution exemplify indirect threats.

*Chicago in Flames: The Rush for Life over Randolph Street Bridge* from *Harper's Weekly* (1871). **Sketch by John R. Chapin.**
Source: iStockphoto.com/ZU_09.

There have been direct consequences of uncontrolled development throughout human history. In 1666, some 13,200 homes were destroyed and over 100,000 people left homeless when a fire ravaged London for three days. In 1871, the Great Chicago Fire, also three days long, killed hundreds of people and burned four square miles of the city. The flammable building materials, inadequate land use planning, and lack of coordinated emergency services exacerbated the harm. With better building materials, thoughtful building placement, and stronger provisions for public infra-structure, such threats can be reduced and tragedy averted. Many building codes that minimize harm to humans were implemented only after a tragedy caused by unregulated construction and development. Yet we continue to develop land in the path of known hazards. Development in floodplains has produced disastrous results. In the Great Flood of 1993, the Missouri River breached levees, destroyed vast highways and whole towns, left thousands homeless, and killed 47 people. In 2005, Hurricane Katrina flooded New Orleans and caused $81.2 billion in damages. The flooding was extensive because the levees failed to keep the waters of Lake Pontchartrain in Louisiana from flowing into the low-lying areas of the city. In what has become almost a yearly ritual in the arid West, homes are destroyed by wildfires and landslides.

Indirect threats to human health include diseases such as cholera, tuberculosis, typhus, and the plague that can be spread by development that lacks adequate sewage facilities, access to clean drinking water, and air circulation. Allowing noxious facilities near residential areas exposes residents to a host of ills that could be avoided. While mostly a thing of the past in the United States, as of 2007 there were still large, unregulated areas in Texas where developers could sell land to the poor with inadequate water and sewer infrastructure (Eckholm 2007). As a result, one resident's well may be located only feet from a neighbor's outhouse.

Other common indirect threats include the contamination of drinking water and air by industrial pollutants; soil erosion from unsustainable farming practices; salinization of cropland; flooding; and habitat destruction. Illegal dumping of toxic waste; soil and water contamination from dry cleaners, gas stations, and factories; and PCB contamination in rivers are all modern examples of how development can degrade the environment with significant consequences for human health.

In the case of the hypothetical Discordia, neighbors and environmental groups raise concerns about the proposed commercial use and the construction process. They rely on Discordia's laws to protect residents against threats to safety such as leaking dumpsters, commercial traffic near schools, and noise levels from construction and operation. The stakeholders ask many questions. Will the project be compatible with existing uses? How will contaminated soil and groundwater be remediated? Where will dumpsters be located? Will truck traffic endanger students? Will there be enough parking? Is the infrastructure (e.g., water, sewer, and roads) adequate to meet the needs of this project? What time of day will construction begin and end? How long will it last? What roads will trucks travel on? How will water running off the site be managed? Will the adjacent stream be protected?

## Development Must Produce Benefits

The second obvious goal of a development project is that it must produce a profit or benefit to the community. Construction and property upkeep require time, money, and resources, and therefore must justify the investment. The profit or community benefit resulting from the construction provides such a justification.

In the Discordia project, the land is currently underutilized. The existing building has been vacant for years, is an eyesore, and is not producing tax revenues for the town. Redevelopment will require an investment of time and money. Buildings must be renovated or demolished, environmental contamination must be remediated, building permits and approvals must be obtained, and new buildings must be designed and built. The ultimate use of the property must, in some way, justify the investment needed to do all this work. Typically, the justification is found in the revenues from the new use that will, over time, exceed the cost of developing the property.

The landowners of the defunct mall must determine if the new, mixed-use project will generate sufficient revenue to pay off the investment of time, effort, and money. The developers must consider future market conditions, future demand, and other external factors. They must also consider the costs of managing the approvals process, preparing land, buying materials, hiring labor, and dealing with public opposition. Conducting an environmental due diligence investigation can cost hundreds of thousands of dollars. In most situations, that expense must be paid off over time by revenue generated from the development. With help from financial institutions and government, a host of potential investment options are available to provide the necessary financial resources for developments. The most popular form of financial support is the "deficit financing" model, in which investors loan the developer money to pay for acquisition of land and construction; this money is then paid back over years with revenues generated from the development. In constrained economic times, financiers are careful to ensure their risks, and exposures are commensurate with the potential financial viability and benefit of the project.

In some developments, revenue is not the ultimate goal. Instead, the goal may be to provide a community benefit, such as building a post office, a monument, a recreational field, a firehouse, a community center, or a work of public art. In these situations, the development costs are typically covered by grants or donations that do not have to be repaid. The funds may be provided by the government, a foundation, or a philanthropist. In either context, deficit financing shows how development decisions are driven by a host of issues beyond local zoning, and each of these must be considered when designing the decision-making processes. In short, the rationale for development is driven by some form of profit to the owners (and investors) and a mix of projected benefits to the community.

## Decisions Must Satisfy Due Process

Due process, the legal term for a fair process, ensures that people are treated fairly and that no party is given a procedural advantage. At its core, due process balances the protection of individual rights and the advancement of public welfare, accounting for the rights of both the landowner and the citizens.

The foundation of due process in the United States builds on similar protections found in England's Magna Carta issued in the thirteenth century. The Magna Carta required that the king adopt laws in accordance with "due process of law" to prevent the king (the government) from altering processes for special people or from making decisions that negatively affected citizens' life, liberty, or property (Mashaw 1985). The concept of due process in the United States gets its legal force through the Fifth and Fourteenth Amendments of the U.S. Constitution and through many Supreme Court rulings.

---

**Box 2.1**

### Due Process and the Discordia Mall

The citizens of Discordia and the developer of the mall have concerns with due process. Citizens want to know that the future of the site will not be decided without a fair hearing and that their needs will be given adequate consideration. Similarly, the developers want to know that the existing laws will be honored and that their investment of time and money will be worthwhile.

However, both the school parents and the neighboring apart-ment residents feel left out. The official notice of the application went to the school board and the owner of the apartment complex, but not to the parents or the apartment tenants. The fact that official, required notice was not provided to them raises their suspicion that

---

their input is not valued and will not be considered. Notice of this sort—to the owners but not others affected by the decision—satisfies due process according to the law, but it may not satisfy the community's notion of fairness. This creates concerns that could be avoided. The legitimate fears the stakeholders have about the project are now compounded by concerns about the fairness of the process.

The perception of fairness often depends on the perspective of the stakeholder. Government regulation can be viewed as providing protection and empowering people to make decisions and take risks. For example, the first zoning ordinance in the United States was created in 1916 in response to lobbying from merchants along New York's Fifth Avenue who were seeking protection of their property investments. Industrial activity in the nearby garment district was starting to encroach on Fifth Avenue. The merchants found that delivery trucks, workers in the streets, and noisy machinery diminished their ability to produce and sell their goods. The high-end customers were offended by the industrial activity, so the Fifth Avenue merchants lobbied city hall to pass a law forbidding industrial uses in the Fifth Avenue shopping district. This zoning law was welcomed by the merchants because it protected their investments and properties.

However, in other situations people resent zoning restrictions because they perceive them as interfering with their right to use their property in any manner they choose. Farmers may be frustrated by laws that restrict what they can build or how they can farm their land. Merchants may bristle at regulations restricting the type of signage they can use and limiting sidewalk displays. A landowner may be shocked to learn that a local wetlands law prevents the construction of a swimming pool.

Residents can also find fault with how the decision is made. In order for a decision to be successful, it must satisfy the legal requirements of due process as well as the community's sense of fairness. If the decision does not meet both the legal and fairness due process thresholds, it may be challenged and its implementation hampered.

**Flatiron Building at Broadway and Fifth Avenue, Manhattan, New York (2012).**
Source: iStockphoto/ferrantraite.

Legal challenges based on procedural grounds are more likely to succeed than challenges based on substantive grounds. When reviewing the actions of local governments and their agencies, courts generally overturn decisions only if they are arbitrary, capricious, or beyond the authority of the board. Judges are reluctant to substitute their opinion for that of the local government. For instance, if a local government denies development in a protected wetland, has the authority to do so, bases that decision on sound evidence, and follows the required procedures, few courts will overturn the decision.

However, courts can, and frequently do, invalidate local decisions when the board fails to follow proper procedure. When determining whether an approach complies with due process requirements, courts look to the state statutes enabling local, land use decision making, local laws, and limitations imposed by federal laws and the Constitution. There are many examples where courts invalidate development decisions because information in the public notice was inaccurate, it did not go to the right property owners, or the required time frame for making a decision was not followed.

---

**Box 2.2**

**Failure to Follow Statutory Procedures Invalidates Countywide Zoning Ordinance**

County commissioners in Buncombe County, North Carolina, enacted an ordinance to regulate multifamily dwellings. A landowner brought suit to challenge the ordinance, arguing that the county did not follow the proper statutory requirements when adopting the ordinance. In reviewing the record, the court found that the county did not comply with the requirements for submitting zoning maps to the planning board. Because the ordinance was not passed in accordance with the statutory requirements, the law was invalidated. (*Thrash Ltd. Partnership v. County of Buncombe*, 673 S.E.2d 706 [N.C. Ct. App. 2009])

---

Understanding how procedural challenges can be used to overturn a board's decision explains why boards are often so concerned with following the proper procedure. It also explains why they may be reluctant to consider supplemental procedures needed to create a mutual gains approach. Due process failures typically arise in the following three situations and can lead to judicial findings that due process has been violated.

- A government may adopt an ordinance through a flawed procedure. For example, the board may fail to conduct an environmental review, neglect to provide adequate notice for a public hearing, or fail to meet the requirements of open meeting laws. These procedural errors make the board's decision vulnerable to being overturned through a legal challenge.
- A government may follow proper procedures when adopting an ordinance, but may go beyond its delegated authority. In this instance, a local government may decide to limit the location of mobile homes on aesthetic grounds. If the state legislature never authorized local governments to restrict development based on aesthetic concerns, such an action would be beyond their authority.
- A law may have been enacted properly, may be in conformance with delegated governmental authority, but may violate due process as applied to an individual landowner. To illustrate, the government may violate a landowner's due process right by denying an application without proper justification or in violation of the governing law. In these situations, the landowner may have a case for a violation of procedural due process.

Some government actions are not legal violations of due process, but they still violate a community's notion of fairness. The proper procedures may be followed, but the public may believe that the government abused its discretion by either denying or approving a particularly controversial development. In situations where notions of fairness, not legal standards, are violated, the cure is political, not judicial. The opponents of an unfair decision may initiate a political campaign to elect a new group of leaders. Either way, due process as both a legal requirement and a public expectation is an important component of development disputes.

This distinction between what is a legal process and what is a fair process is very important in controversial decisions. A fair process is more likely to be effective in controversial decisions than a process that meets only the minimal legal requirements. In the Discordia example, while existing laws designate permissible uses for this parcel, it is conceivable that some other use may be more appropriate. In fact, the applicant is proposing commercial office space on the second floor. This use is not allowed in this zone. The legal process to approve new uses is called "rezoning." When deciding to rezone or not, Discordia must use a process that satisfies legal due process. However, the board must also use a process that is perceived as fair by all of the stakeholders. If the board goes through the legal procedures that satisfy due process yet the neighbors do not feel included or heard, the neighbors are likely to voice their disappointment and oppose the decision through political or legal challenges. In these situations, a controversial decision can spiral out of control unless the board uses procedures that satisfy the interested parties' sense of fairness.

## HOW THE REQUIRED PROCESS ACCOMMODATES THE MUTUAL GAINS APPROACH

A common misperception among land use boards is that the required process sets a ceiling limiting what procedures can be adopted. When board members think about what processes they *must* use according to law, this becomes conflated with what processes they *can* use. In reality, the required process specifies only the *minimum* procedure, not the *maximum*. For example, when making land use decisions, the board must hold a public hearing, the applicant must provide notice to the adjacent property owners, and the government must make a decision within a given time frame. These are all minimum requirements. However, the government can still suggest or require additional procedures to supplement, not replace, the required process. The mutual gains approach can be used before, during, and after the legally required process and can satisfy both due process legal requirements and notions of fairness.

To illustrate, some governments employ mutual gains approaches before the required process is triggered; midway after the required process has begun; and after a decision has been made (see figure 2.1). They may take the form of preapplication procedures, expanded notice provisions that include a greater number of stakeholders, and extensive informational

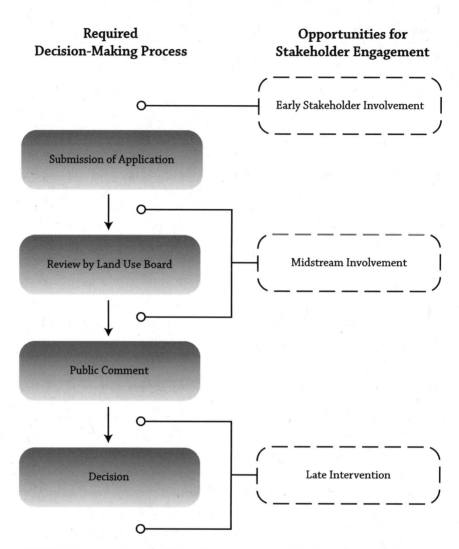

**Required Decision-Making Process**

**Opportunities for Stakeholder Engagement**

Early Stakeholder Involvement

Submission of Application

Review by Land Use Board

Midstream Involvement

Public Comment

Decision

Late Intervention

**FIGURE 2.1 Integrating the Mutual Gains Approach into the Required Process**

meetings far beyond what is required at public hearings. For example, the town of Dover, New York, requires special permit applicants to submit a conceptual plan of their proposed development to the zoning enforcement officer or ZEO (Dover, NY, 1999). This provision gives the town the opportunity to screen applications before they enter the process. The ZEO who sees an application that is likely to be controversial can suggest that the applicant consider a supplemental mutual gains effort right from the beginning. This preapplication procedure can short-circuit the spiral of unmanaged conflict discussed in chapter 3.

Tucson, Arizona, has a similar local law requiring applicants to convene a preapplication meeting with neighbors (Tucson, AZ 2004). This law states that the municipality values dialogue before the required process begins. Similar programs exist in cities such as Albuquerque, New Mexico; Berkeley, California; Bozeman, Montana; Denver and Colorado Springs, Colorado; and states such as Georgia, Hawaii, and Minnesota.

Supplementing the required process can also occur after the preapplication stage has passed. For example, many communities have used the environmental review process to expand stakeholder involvement. Most environmental review statutes have a process to determine the scope of review to decide what issues will be studied. The mutual gains processes can be used to involve citizens in those scoping decisions. This may involve stakeholders in the middle of the required process. Similarly, robust design workshops, such as charrettes, can be used during the approval process to increase stakeholder involvement.

The mutual gains approach can also be used after a decision has been made, and even after a decision has been appealed. In Massachusetts, parties who appeal local, conservation commission decisions are offered an opportunity to mediate before being heard by a judge. Similar programs exist in California, Connecticut, Florida, Maine, North Carolina, South Carolina, Vermont, and Washington.

While the mutual gains approach can be used at any stage, employing it later can be more difficult. After battling for advantage in the required decision-making process, the amount of misinformation can be confusing, relationships among the parties may be strained, and the focus may have shifted from solving the problem (coming up with a satisfying land use decision) to defeating the other side. In addition, at this late point parties may not have the same amount of time, money, and patience as they did at the beginning of the process. For this reason, communities that supplement the process in the early stages are more likely to be successful and less likely to need the help of professional facilitators and mediators. Conversely, communities looking to use mutual gains approaches later in the process are more likely to need a professional mediator to overcome the barriers that have been built. Figure 2.2 illustrates this inverse

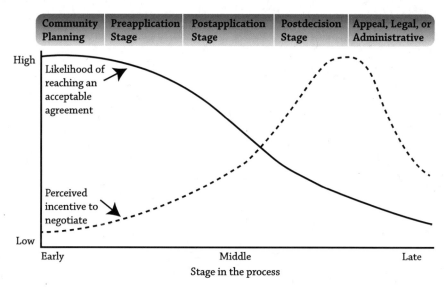

| Community Planning | Preapplication Stage | Postapplication Stage | Postdecision Stage | Appeal, Legal, or Administrative |
|---|---|---|---|---|

**FIGURE 2.2  Relationship Between the Incentive to Negotiate and the Likelihood of Reaching an Agreement**

relationship between the incentive to negotiate and the likelihood of reaching agreement.

■  ■  ■

Understanding the required land use decision-making process is the first step toward making better process choices. Stakeholders will be better equipped to navigate the barriers to implementing mutual gains approaches if they understand the difference between what is legally required and what is supplemental.

Land use decision-making boards have a difficult task. They are charged with protecting the rights of landowners as well as the community; they must balance the protection of community resources and the protection of property rights. They are obligated to follow legally mandated procedures that protect their decisions from adverse judicial rulings. In many instances, the existing process creates conflicting priorities and raises questions of fairness. Has the board already made up its mind? Is the board in the pocket of the developer? Has it already decided to deny an application? A mutual gains approach can address these concerns by shifting from an adversarial, decision-making process to a creative, information-sharing process focused on the underlying needs and interests of the stakeholders.

Significant land use decisions need not deteriorate into unproductive battles. The required process can be supplemented with the mutual gains approach to provide opportunities for stakeholders to work together creatively to generate ideas and options. We do not need to settle for processes that destroy value, relationships, and community through divisive conflict. The following chapters provide a structure and a framework to break this cycle.

# CHAPTER 3

■ ■ ■ ☐ ☐ ☐ ☐ ☐ ☐

# Conflict and Land Use

Why is it that across the United States, regardless of geography, political affiliation, economic status, or type of development, land use decision making seems to bring citizens, developers, and competing advocacy groups to loggerheads?

Local planning and zoning commissions are faced with divergent interests without a clear path for reconciliation or compromise. Despite their sophisticated designs, charts, graphs, and engineering analyses, project proponents often stand helpless before an angry crowd. Citizens often feel powerless as monied interests from outside of their community propose significant and, in their view, adverse changes. Environmental and conservation groups fear that each new acre of developed land is forever lost for habitat, threatened species, and water quality protection. Property rights advocates watch as parties with no financial stake tread upon the individual rights of property owners to use and enjoy their property.

This chapter explores the many reasons that land use decisions often result in conflict. The discussion begins with an example of a land use dispute in an urban redevelopment neighborhood to highlight the complexities of land use conflict in the United States. It describes the sources of conflict, including the impacts on the quality of life, the environment, and fiscal health.

## ASSEMBLY SQUARE: A CASE STUDY

In 1998, Assembly Square in Somerville, Massachusetts, was called the best development site left in Greater Boston for high-density development (Shutkin 2001). The large brownfield area had decayed since the 1960s when automobile and other heavy manufacturing industries closed. However, the site was still extraordinarily well supported by public infrastructure, including local roads and highways, an adjacent track of the Massachusetts Bay Transit Authority train, and three longer-distance commuter rail lines coming in and out of downtown Boston. The site had waterfront property along the Mystic River and sat just 15 minutes from Boston's financial and commercial centers, Logan International Airport, and the main campuses of Harvard University and MIT.

An attempt to revitalize the area in the late 1970s resulted in the construction of a shopping mall, but after a brief flurry of activity, the mall fell into decline and the rest of the area remained either undeveloped or a hodgepodge of small manufacturing, commercial, and retail companies. Somerville's hopes that new office space and a hotel would follow the construction of the mall were thwarted as the site became best known for its frequent car thefts rather than as a new source of jobs and tax revenue for the city.

In the late 1990s, two distinct visions for the area began to emerge. On one side, the consortium of developers who owned the land were putting together plans to construct two big-box stores—a Home Depot and an IKEA—and the parking lots and roads to support them. Meanwhile, a group of local citizens, including neighbors and representatives of environmental and economic development interests, had coalesced in a group called the Mystic View Task Force (Task Force). The Task Force wanted to promote smart growth principles for future development of Assembly Square, including mixed use, walkability, access to public transit, and open space. Unlike many opponents of development, the Task Force was a proponent of a very specific kind of development and, interestingly, for more, not less, density. At first the Task Force was supported by State Representative Pat Jehlen, as well as by Somerville mayor Dorothy Kelly Gay, and the developers complied with requests from the city to delay development until a professional planning firm could draft a comprehensive master plan for the area.

The firm hired by the city produced a controversial document that tried (and failed) to meet all of the stakeholders' interests. They recommended a 20-year, phased approach that allowed the big-box developments to proceed immediately, with the understanding that development around the retail giants over the following years could incorporate features that matched the longer-term vision of dense, multiuse, transit-oriented development the citizens envisioned. The planning firm suggested that over time the larger stores would phase out naturally as real estate values grew and higher-density uses became more economically feasible.

Not surprisingly, the developers supported this plan, but the Task Force did not. The citizens and other representatives did not believe that this plan would turn over from car-accessible, large-scale stores to the smaller-scale, transit-oriented vision they had for the long term. However, the Task Force was not blind to the need for immediate economic growth and job creation, which the phased strategy offered. The Task Force's efforts switched focus to prove the feasibility of smart growth development in the short term, rather than simply as an aspiration for the future.

The developers proceeded, nonetheless, with their permit applications to the city, although they previously had been rejected. The mayor and her administration, following the proposal the planning professionals provided, approved the permit requests. The Task Force felt forced to pursue legal action, and the next several years were lost to litigation. The conflict led to the mayor losing her position. Neighbor was pitted against neighbor about the taxes lost to the city, the fiscal realities of constrained budgets, and the desire for the city to grow out of its long-standing "second rate" status as compared to the adjacent Cambridge.

## SOURCES OF LAND USE CONFLICT

Land is intimately connected to peoples' livelihoods, sense of self and community, and health and well-being. Because of this, serious conflicts around land use can be expected. As presented in the Assembly Square case, and in many land use cases in general, sources of conflict range from quality-of-life issues to environmental impacts to conflicting visions for the future.

### Quality-of-Life Issues

Impacts on the quality of life are usually direct and relatively immediate, and they affect public health and safety, including traffic, noise, light, odor, and aesthetics. For example, noise is caused by a runway expansion at a local airport. Increased traffic is caused by a new office building, a new residential subdivision, or a concentration of new businesses around a highway interchange. There are the shadows and wind effects of large buildings in urban environments. With any land use change, someone will be affected, perceptions of the impacts will differ widely, and the land use system must thus try to arbitrate between these competing interests and needs.

Often the extent, severity, and cause of these quality-of-life impacts are in dispute. In the Assembly Square case, the developers maintained that there was only benefit in the proposed development. After all, what could be worse than a crime-ridden, empty, derelict parcel of land? But many argued the opposite. The new development would increase traffic substantially. The big-box stores would not create an exciting, new urban neighborhood, but a vast sea of asphalt, cars, and dull building design. The site, adjacent to the Mystic River, would not be a venue for waterfront revitalization, but rather the big-box stores would face away from this important natural feature and essentially block most visual and physical access to the water.

Take the controversy that arose in the city of West Chester, Pennsylvania, where growing signs of socioeconomic stress led local charitable foundations to form a nonprofit shelter, Safe Harbor of Greater West Chester, to provide meals and counseling for the homeless. For two winters in the early 1990s, Safe Harbor operated a temporary shelter. A different church hosted the shelter each month in order to avoid permit requirements that would otherwise have been imposed by the county government. During this time, Safe Harbor evaluated several potential sites for a permanent facility and, in 1994, found an abandoned downtown garage that had the space necessary to serve its needs. However, local business owners were alarmed at the prospect of a downtown shelter and felt deeply frustrated by the fact that a shelter might be allowed under existing zoning. Owners worried about the effects on patronage of their businesses and were concerned about how the shelter would alter perceptions of the area. The concerns cited included public safety, potential violence, antisocial behavior, and other "undesirable" behaviors. They fought hard to prevent the site from being converted into a shelter. Eventually, a mediator was brought in to help the parties identify areas of agreement and discuss options for the site. In the end, agreement was reached about what would be appropriate and the facility was approved.

## Environmental Impacts

Land use conflict is frequently driven by concerns about ecosystem protection and the longer-term, indirect impacts that include damage to wetlands, habitats, floodplains, species, and water quality, among others. These environmental issues raise broad questions about the effect of the proposal not merely on the site but also on the surrounding resources, for instance watersheds, wetlands delineation, and 100-year floodplains.

The environmental impacts of a particular action may play out over several generations and often include complex issues, uncertainties, and parameters. The Assembly Square case raised strong concerns about air quality and environmental justice. The site was already plagued by a busy highway with huge amounts of rush hour traffic contributing to both standard pollutants (ozone, NOx, SOx) and air toxics into the surrounding low- to modest-income neighborhoods. In addition, citizens were concerned that the highly automobile-dependent uses such as big-box stores would discourage the development of sorely needed mass transit options and the project would simply contribute more to congestion and air pollution.

Controversies around the construction of wind turbines provide another rich example: How does one consider the visual effects on viewsheds, the noise impacts on abutters, the construction impacts of road work around the turbines, and the effects on wildlife (particularly birds and bats), compared with the long-term need for lower-carbon energy to mitigate global climate change? In New England, the siting of wind turbines tends to be contentious, pitting environmental and conservation allies against one another. Some conservation groups fight proposals that might impact remote ridges, wildlife corridors, and forests. Other environmental groups support wind technology development and argue that local landscape and environmental impacts are less onerous than the threat of climate change, the use of fossil fuels, or the impacts other communities experience from other kinds of energy extraction and production, such as mountaintop removal for coal mining.

## Fiscal Impacts

Land development has fiscal impacts on towns, cities, and taxpayers. In the United States, where many people have ambivalent views of taxes, fiscal impacts of development have become a significant bone of contention. For example, while many may not oppose additional housing development, some citizens and advocates argue that residential development places an increased burden on existing taxpayers. Increased municipal costs due to new, single-use residential development and the need for sewer, water, public safety services, and schools may not be offset by the tax revenues generated by a given development. For Assembly Square, the proponents argued that redevelopment in the short term would generate much-needed tax revenue for a city with a very high burden on residential taxpayers and would create high-paying construction jobs and longer-term retail opportunities. For opponents, the big-box stores would generate modest tax revenues at best, which would be offset by the detrimental effects of traffic and other issues. A mixed-use, walkable, transit-oriented development, the Task Force argued, would be far more dense, generate many more construction jobs due to the density of construction, create additional tax revenue, and be more sustainable over the long term.

Many studies of the costs of community services (e.g., education, trash removal, and road maintenance) have been completed across a number of locales and states. These studies were originally conducted by land trusts to identify the hidden costs of residential development versus farm and open space protection. The authors of a meta-analysis of community service costs across some 125 studies stated, "We find clear support for the common perception that residential land uses tend to have ratios greater than one, while commercial/industrial and agricultural/open-space land uses tend to have ratios less than one. In short, residential development does not pay for itself, while commercial or industrial development does" (Kotchen and Schulte 2009). Thus, land development does not merely pose physical problems, it may also impose inequitable and meaningful fiscal impacts on individual taxpayers.

In addition to residential property development, many cities have competed actively for manufacturing plants, sports stadiums, and other forms of economic development. Often, cities and towns have been willing to offer substantial tax relief in the hope of drawing new anchors of growth and vitality. But, with stadiums as an example, the cost of the tax relief to the stadium owners often exceeds the estimated value of financial gain through local jobs and increased spending.

## Fragmented and Competing Jurisdictions

The sheer number of local towns, villages, cities, and counties in the United States makes local land use complex and fragmented. Unlike federal agencies, which have the Administrative Procedure Act (APA) to guide decision-making processes, little overarching legislation guides administrative procedures of local entities. Under municipal law, "the legislative body of a municipality is said to have inherent power to make its own rules of procedure so long as these are not violative of the constitution, state statutes, or the municipality's own charter" (Reynolds 2001, 215). While federal government land management agencies with their more consistent and consolidated rules and regulations are not without conflict, the fragmented nature of local land use control of private and municipal lands makes for a rich, complex patchwork of local idiosyncrasies, politics, rules, and regulations. Each municipality has its own process for approval, its own special conditions, and its own unique ordinances, sometimes completely different from those of adjacent jurisdictions. While this system preserves local autonomy and independence, it also creates a complex maze of unique rules and regulations for developers, consultants, and citizens to navigate.

A number of jurisdictional issues may drive conflict when one agency does not have full authority over a site or project. A golf course application may span two or three municipalities. A decision on the border of one town may impose impacts or costs on an adjacent town. A major development such as a casino might have regional impacts on affordable housing, traffic, businesses, and so forth. Though land use decisions are local, they can have regional impacts that involve additional jurisdictional authorities such as regional planning bodies or transportation and environmental agencies, creating both complexity and conflict.

In the Assembly Square case, the developers had to work through the planning board, the zoning board of appeals, and the city council, all within the city. Because mass transit would be essential to the ultimate success of the site, the city and developers also had to engage the regional transit authority as well as the state government. Developers had to contend with specific state tidal regulations and special environmental review because the site was in a tidal wetland.

In the small state of Delaware, planning is done locally, though the governor's office initiatives encourage development around statewide goals regarding transit-oriented and higher-density development. But in New Castle County, the most populous county in Delaware, review and approval of all transportation issues is done by the state's department of transportation. Transportation modeling, road cuts, and the regional impact are reviewed and approved by the state, often confusing citizens and developers as to where the permit application stands and why the approval process takes so long.

## Procedural and Institutional Issues

Numerous procedural issues further increase land use conflict. Due to the idiosyncratic and parochial nature of local land use decision making, the public may fear favoritism, backroom deals, and other biases as development applications make their way through the process. In Assembly Square, for instance, one of the complaints of local residents and their advocates was their exclusion from key, local decision-making processes. Residential abutters to the site complained they had little influence over the city's headlong charge into the development. They especially did not like the fact that the city controlled one of the parcels and did not conduct an open bidding process to select the developer. Residents raged against a city government that they felt was nonresponsive and tainted by decades of bribes and improper relationships. City officials claimed that regardless of how they tried to accommodate citizens' needs, the imperatives for the right kind of economic development were too great.

In the face of such institutional and procedural distrust, there is a shared interest in finding a more inclusive approach to prevent a backlash from closed-door processes. Members of the public increasingly seek more transparency, accountability, and openness. Current laws usually require advance notice of meetings and the public availability of certain documents. As described in chapter 2, participation, notice, and information also raise "fairness" concerns about whether those affected by a decision have full opportunity to participate in local decisions.

Some towns actively address procedural challenges in the land use planning process. Falmouth, Maine, an upscale suburban community adjacent to the city of Portland, heard concerns over its complicated, multicommittee, land use planning process. In response, Falmouth retained the Consensus Building Institute (CBI) to help improve the process. An electronic survey sent to multiple email lists generated responses from local citizens about how they perceived their process of land use decision making. When asked to describe the Town of Falmouth's land use system in one word, some said proactive, innovative, progressive, high quality, and strategic. Others described the system as heavy, complicated, broken, disorganized, poorly coordinated, unpredictable, and unfriendly to land owners. These divergent views are commonplace and are often the reasons behind land use conflicts.

## The Constitution and the Meaning of Private Property

Private property is one of the essential foundations of Western market economies. It is a deeply embedded concept in the United States that means different things to different people. The lack of agreement about the extent to which government can limit or infringe upon private property causes ongoing conflict throughout the country.

*Kelo v. City of New London* (Connecticut) is a recent Supreme Court case that sought to delineate the boundaries of government action versus private property rights. The city of New London, faced with a declining military presence, sought new sources of economic development. Working in partnership with private developers, it planned to assemble a group of land parcels, including many individually owned lots on which homes were built, for the development of a five-star hotel and other facilities. These lots were adjacent to a major pharmaceutical company's proposed research and development headquarters. Susette Kelo was one of the affected homeowners. The city, through a separate economic development corporation, moved on the homeowners through eminent domain (a government's ability under the Constitution to take a property for public purpose in exchange for fair market compensation). Ms. Kelo filed a lawsuit challenging the taking, and the case ultimately made its way to the U.S. Supreme Court, which issued a controversial, five-to-four decision in favor of the city.

The central legal issue was whether or not the government had the right to use eminent domain against private property owners for a purpose that was not directly tied to the public infrastructure (e.g., the building of a road). Following that decision, many states passed laws restricting the use of eminent domain for economic development. The case galvanized numerous groups around the rights of private property owners, especially homeowners. Susette Kelo summed it up best in her testimony to Congress: "The battle against eminent domain abuse may have started as a way for me to save my little pink cottage. But it has rightfully grown into something much larger—the fight to restore the American Dream and the sacredness and security of each one of our homes" (Benedict 2009, 2).

## Values and Identities

Land use conflicts are not merely the result of people's concerns about the impacts, costs, and benefits of land use choices. They also arise from the values people hold and their senses of identity. Historic preservation conflicts are often an effort to preserve and restore the town's past, not to visualize what it might become in the future. Local citizens may fight to preserve a small restaurant in the face of competing, new land use proposals because it is a community-gathering place with history, memory, and relationships. In addition, fairness and justice can play a role in land use disputes in situations in which disenfranchised, poor, or minority communities feel that they have been singled out to bear a disproportionate number of local harms, such as energy plants, landfills, and other uses that benefit the larger population at the expense of a few.

Ultimately, many land use conflicts are driven by deeply held and sometimes irreconcilable value differences. Do people value open ridgelines on their hills or renewable energy and self-sufficiency that require wind farms to be erected on those ridges? Are wind turbines beautiful or ugly? Is open space more important than affordable housing? Should a Muslim cultural center be built near the site of the World Trade Center? What would be the impact of an amusement park near the battlefields of Gettysburg? Should people be allowed to rebuild their homes along storm-ravaged coasts after a major hurricane? We addressed such divergent value differences when we facilitated a dispute over permitting off-road driving on a seashore area. The residents expressed that losing the opportunity to drive on the beach would be to lose the place where families built memories together, where the pleasures of fishing, relaxing, and watching the sunrise would be eliminated, and where a deep connection to a place and ones' identity would be severed. Thus, land use becomes not merely an issue of interest, but of identity. In the United States, land and home are sacrosanct and, in part, what make us Americans.

## Defining Community

Land use is not merely a debate about physical space or economics; it involves a stand on who we are and what we want our communities to be. Residents may not want their Main Street replaced by a strip mall on the edge of town. They want their town's gateway to be open and bucolic, not dense and commercial. Such conflicts can seem clanish in the sense that communities are focused on defining who belongs and who does not belong in the community. For example, a developer once said to one of us, "I go to site a Walmart, and the opposition comes out of the woodwork. I go to site a Target, with the exact same traffic and other impacts, and I can't build it fast enough to make people happy!"

In this way, fiscal impact conflicts can tap into deep-seated, economic anxiety and strong differences among socioeconomic classes. In the far South Side of Chicago, in the late 2000s, residents in the Ninth Ward were equally divided about a proposed development that included Walmart as an anchor tenant. Some argued that Walmart would spur economic development in a community devoid of good jobs and that it could provide low-cost goods, particularly groceries, in a town that lacked access to healthier food. Others argued that low-wage jobs would not provide sufficient income, workers could not unionize, and small, local mom-and-pop shops would be driven out of business. As one resident said in favor of the proposal, "It suddenly came upon us that this was the offer: You can have a WalMart, or you're not gonna have anything there" (Melendez 2010).

One of the more famous land use cases that involved community and fair housing began in the 1970s. During this time, many proponents of affordable housing concluded that large lot sizes and other zoning rules were often intentionally implemented to exclude people with low and moderate incomes from obtaining housing in municipalities, especially affluent suburbs of major metropolitan areas. Mount Laurel, New Jersey, was one such community. The case made its way twice to the New Jersey Supreme Court with the court ruling in favor of the plaintiffs by finding the zoning unconstitutional under the state's constitution (Nolon 1986). Because this ruling would not address the statewide problem, this issue required an act of the New Jersey legislature to resolve the matter. At the heart of the case were several questions: What does it mean to be a community? Can you exclude some, not directly by race, but de facto by income? If so, is this discrimination? Furthermore, is the very character of your community compromised by making it financially difficult for teachers, firefighters, and other employees to live where they work? On the other hand, if you cannot define your community (and in practice, defining community means leaving some out and including others), is the desirability of the homes and community threatened? Affordable housing is one of the many issues raised in the land use context that speak to, and sometimes tear at, the very heart of what it means to be a community.

## Uncertainty and the Future

No stakeholder can predict the future of the local economy; the value of certain kinds of land uses; changes in public tastes, demographics, and values; or even what climate a proposed development might have to withstand in the future. Land use decisions are also complicated by the fact that they can and may shape an uncertain future. Land use decisions by their nature are long-term decisions; a building may stand for a human lifetime, or longer. A comprehensive plan seeks to shape development over decades. While land use decision making assumes much of the financial risk is the developer's to bear, the community may bear the consequences of poor decisions in the long term. Thus, the uncertainty of the impact of the long-term decisions explains the intensity and complexity of many land use disputes.

## Communications and Cognitive Biases

A number of communication and conceptual challenges also cause conflict. Administrative procedures, formal presentations, and strict adherence to *Robert's Rules of Order* (the procedures most civic organizations use to guide meetings) may cause confusion, impede clarity on key issues, and jeopardize relationships. Volunteers without much experience or training in managing productive hearings often staff local boards and are therefore unequipped to effectively communicate with the residents. Citizens may object as much to the lack of communication as to the proposal itself. A terse word or poorly managed interchange in a public meeting can lead to misunderstanding and increased conflict.

The manner in which proposals are presented is also important. Professionally prepared plans and renderings can either convey expertise and competence or indicate slickness and inflexibility, depending on local perceptions and expectations. For example, a visual model of a wind turbine was shown at a local planning board meeting in Manchester, Vermont. The image of the wind turbines on the ridge of a hill was set against a gray, overcast sky, a weather condition all too frequent in the region. A citizen remarked that the visualization was intentionally misleading and that the turbine should be set against a blue sky to show its real visual impact. Is the proponent really minimizing the visual impact of the turbines? Is the opponent merely trying to make the worst case possible? Whatever the case, the act of communication in a contentious setting, if poorly managed, can trigger a series of interactions that can erode trust, muddy the clarity of the information, and prevent full consideration of the case. Communication itself can cause conflict, embedded as it is in roles, interests, and stakes.

Cognitive bias also poses a set of challenges. Over the last 20 years, behavioral economics has shown that we all process information imperfectly and show predictable biases. These biases are known as cognitive biases. They are generally defined as psychological phenomena, processes, and predispositions that inhibit the fully rational consideration of information (DeFlorio and Field 2007).

One common cognitive bias is viewing a land use dispute as a "fixed pie" where no additional value can be added. Parties assume that the pie of benefits or burdens is finite and fixed. Their duty is to carve out as many slices as possible for themselves or for the interests they represent. For example, controversies over riparian buffers (areas set aside from development near waterways to provide natural filtering of storm water, wildlife habitat, and other ecological functions) are common. The establishment of riparian buffers is complex, involving a consideration of slope, vegetated cover, wetlands and streams, and overlap with other laws such as storm water regulations. In general, developers seek to limit areas that are closed to development and environmentalists want to maximize areas set aside for environmental functions, such as sediment capture, nutrient filtering, and wildlife habitat.

However, the issues often become framed in the fixed pie view, as parties argue over the width of the buffer zone, for example, instead of seeing mutual opportunity to design a buffer. In some cases, buffers may add valuable green space and landscaping to a development, increasing property values while providing ecological benefits. Yet, frequently the possibility for trade-offs across issues is lost in the fight over a piece of the pie.

Another important cognitive bias is the notion of interpersonal comparison and relative fairness. A common question in land use decision making is the perception of who is benefiting from a development and who may be bearing the real or perceived costs of it. In general, people show great concern for relative fairness when benefits are being distributed.

How does this cognitive barrier apply to land use? If a developer is receiving a profit or financial benefit that, in a resident's view, far exceeds the benefit to the resident (fees, neighborhood benefits, or taxes), the resident might oppose the proposal. While allocation of benefits overall might be net positive in the planner or developer's view, the relative allocation of those benefits may cause some stakeholders to adamantly oppose what seems to be at least marginally in their best interest.

■ ■ ■

While land use decision making focuses on physical, natural, and built environments, our review of the causes of conflict suggests that land represents a much larger set of economic, personal, and societal issues. Land use conflict reveals deep tensions about who we are as individuals and in what kind of community we wish to live. As discussed throughout this book, established procedures alone are not sufficient to address the most complex cases. People of diverse interests must engage each other to make decisions that satisfy a range of values and concerns.

The Assembly Square case described at the beginning of this chapter is a story with many lessons. In 2006, after years of litigation, an agreement was reached after a yearlong mediation process between the developers and the lead group of opponents in consultation with the city. They arrived at a comprehensive arrangement that demonstrated strategic trading among the many interests to create a package everyone could live with. The IKEA store was approved for construction, but located on an inland parcel rather than along the Mystic River's bank in order to allow greenway development for bike paths, the marina, and social gathering places. The developers committed money to build a subway stop on the site and to perform ongoing traffic monitoring and remediation, as necessary. They also agreed to fund a health impact study, while the city formalized development guidelines, and a transit-oriented master plan for the area. Today, Assembly Row (as it has been rebranded by the developers) is a growing hub of activity.

# PART II ▪ STEPS

# CHAPTER 4

■ ■ ■ ■ □ □ □ □ □

# Assessing and Understanding Stakeholders, Issues, and Interests

The first three chapters covered the basics of the mutual gains approach. This section discusses the following four stages of the approach.

1. Assessing and understanding the stakeholders, issues, and interests (chapter 4)
2. Designing a process for collaboration (chapter 5)
3. Facilitating deliberations (chapter 6)
4. Implementing agreements (chapter 7)

## ASSESSMENTS

To begin applying the mutual gains approach to a land use dispute, the initial intervention is to determine what kind of effort is appropriate under the circumstances. This first step is called an "assessment." This chapter describes the process of assessment, the reasons to consider employing one, the steps involved in conducting an assessment, the benefits that may result, and some options available to those who conduct the assessment.

Consider the hypothetical decision in Discordia. The developer purchased the vacant mall two years ago. As market conditions improved, she filed a development application with the Discordia Planning Board to build new commercial buildings on the site. The developer imagined that most citizens would be thrilled to finally see new activity on the dilapidated site. However, prior to the first formal hearing, opposition has arisen. Over one hundred unhappy citizens attend the first hearing of the planning board on permitting the proposed development.

The developer is taken aback by the level and intensity of the complaints. The attendees ask a litany of questions. Will the project be compatible with existing uses? Will it disturb the neighbors in the Bailey Apartments? Will the traffic endanger children at the Quimby Elementary School? How will the lighting be arranged? Where will dumpsters be located? When will deliveries be made? Will there be enough parking? Is the infrastructure (e.g., water, sewer, and roads) adequate to meet the needs of this project? What time of day will construction begin and end, and how long will it last? On which roads will the trucks travel? If the site is contaminated from previous uses, how will it be cleaned up? How will this affect the wetlands on the edge of the parking lot by Discordia Creek?

The planning board, realizing that the redevelopment of the site is more controversial than expected, asks the city planner to organize additional meetings to work through the issues. The developer reluctantly agrees. Many of the hearing attendees express their delight that the planning board has delayed a decision until more discussions take place. The planner quietly wonders, how can I manage this process effectively?

The planner realizes, given her experience, that no single person or organization is likely to have a complete understanding of all the factors that will go into this decision. Each will have their own perspective, interest, and bias. As described in chapter 3, people are passionate about land, their homes, their community, and their rights. In controversial cases, where the potential to enflame the conflict is high, an assessment can be used to better understand the issues raised by the decision.

Completing the assessment requires deciding who should be involved, what topics should be addressed, and how such a process should be structured. An impartial assessor who gathers information and conducts interviews with all of the stakeholders often carries out the assessment. This person may be a professional mediator or a qualified person from the community. The interviews are summarized in a report with detailed findings and recommendations that is then circulated for comment.

Assessments help both the stakeholders and assessors clarify the options for moving forward, identify the costs and benefits of a collaborative process, and settle on the most appropriate approach to avoid legal challenges, media campaigns, or administrative processes. Assessments produce substantial amounts of information with a relatively small commitment of time from stakeholders. Finally, they offer an overview of the situation by describing the range of stakeholders' perceptions and perspectives, which is very helpful for the later stages of the mutual gains approach.

Assessments can address the following common challenges.

- **Conflicts over the general use of land.** An assessment can be used to help a community develop a vision for how they want to grow. For example, in 2008 the rural Connecticut town of Killingly conducted an assessment to identify the priorities of their community, which they found to be open space, a sense of quiet, and small gathering places (Town of Killingly 2009). The community then began to explore how to encourage dense development in a few key places along their borders in a way that would preserve their priorities.
- **Multiple jurisdictions working together.** Assessments can be used to identify opportunities for neighboring communities to jointly address shared land use challenges such as transportation and affordable housing. In the Rocky Mountain West, a foundation and a nonprofit collaborated to help adjacent communities work together and sponsored an assessment to consider the planning challenges between communities rich in resorts or amenities, such as Telluride, Colorado, and Jackson Hole, Wyoming, and surrounding communities with fewer resources (Consensus Building Institute 2007). The processes included brainstorming issues of mutual concern and assessing seven regions to identify important topics and to learn what types of support might be most useful to assist these communities.
- **Site-specific developments.** When a community is faced with a controversial development project, an assessment can be used to explore alternatives to the typically adversarial process. In the case of a nine-acre site in the university town of Durham, New Hampshire, a facilitation team from the Consensus Building Institute (CBI) met with abutters, environmentalists, the business community, and the local university to determine if a collaborative process could lead to a viable site redevelopment plan (American Institute of Architects 2008). As a result, the parties agreed upon a simple list of issues, committed to a work plan to redevelop the old strip mall, and planned for a mixed-use development and protection of an on-site stream. In addition, the abutters' concerns about the scale, aesthetics, and traffic were addressed. They also

determined how to reconnect the site to the local downtown and university areas. Unfortunately, because of a downturn in the economy, the project has not yet been built.

- ■ *Challenges to the decision process itself.* Sometimes, parties raise questions about the process itself. Is the decision-making process as efficient and fair as it could be? Have too many committees proliferated over time? Does the process assist or hinder economic development? Do all voices get a chance to be heard? Assessments can help answer these questions.

For example, in New Castle County, Delaware, a statewide public policy institute engaged CBI to explore the strengths and weaknesses of the existing land use permitting process (New Castle 2009). The assessment requested feedback on how the land use process might be improved and whether elected officials, developers, and neighborhood activists might jointly explore improvements to the permitting process.

## ESSENTIAL STEPS IN CONFLICT ASSESSMENT

The primary components of effective assessment have been tested and refined over the past few decades by professional mediators and facilitators. A detailed description of the seven primary steps in an assessment, the actions to be taken, the decisions to be made, and the questions they answer follows.

---

**Box 4.1**

**Basic Steps in Assessment**

1. Initiate an assessment.
2. Design the assessment.
3. Interview stakeholders.
4. Analyze and present the findings.
5. Decide whether to proceed.
6. Design the process.
7. Share the results.

---

While these steps are listed here in a linear fashion, the latter steps often occur simultaneously. For example, an assessment team might share results (step 7) while still finalizing the findings (step 4) and beginning to design the assessment process (step 6). In another situation, it might be crucial to make a decision about whether to proceed with a collaborative process (step 5) while written materials are shared, requiring that steps 5, 6, and 7 occur concurrently.

## Step 1: Initiate an Assessment

If an assessment is deemed appropriate, the search begins for a capable and trusted assessor.

- ■ *Who Should Convene an Assessment?* The convener may be the local planning department, an elected official, the town or city council, or a group of citizens, but they must have some authority, legitimacy, and financial resources. At times, citizens and developers have convened an assessment on their own, but ultimately land use decision makers are always brought on board at some point. Who convenes the assessment is very important as it will determine how the results are viewed by those involved. For example, if a developer is the sole convener of an assessment, the process may be viewed skeptically by neighbors and local officials.

  Most often, a government entity, such as a local planning department or elected board, retains the assessor. The town may convene the assessment, but hire an independent, neutral, mediator to act as the assessor to protect confidentiality and provide an unbiased explanation of process choices. However, there are situations in which the convener is also the assessor. For example, a town may convene an assessment and enlist the planning staff to conduct it. In Discordia, the planning board acts as the convener because it is the decision-making board with authority over the project. The mall redevelopment will require a conditional use permit and the planning board makes those decisions in Discordia. Most important, though, is that the convener meets the following basic criteria.

- ■ *Be open to influence*. Be viewed as open to ideas that may emerge during the process.

- *Be legitimate*. Have the sufficient authority, trust, and support of participants to lend credibility to the process.
- *Be influential*. Be able to encourage and compel participation in the process.

---

### Box 4.2

**Convener's Considerations**

- Where are we in the process?
- How long do we expect the process to last?
- Have we identified the stakeholders?
- Have there been previous attempts at dispute resolution?
- What are the stakeholders' alternatives to negotiation?
- Could new information, players, or opportunities change the dynamics of the conflict at this time? How?
- Do we have the resources to support an appropriately scaled analysis?
- What else do we need to know to determine what should happen next?

---

- *Who Carries Out the Assessment?* Ideally, the convener will select a competent and neutral party to serve as the assessor. Depending on the circumstances, the assessor may be a local planner, a trusted and capable citizen or group of citizens, or a mediator from the community. They may be hired or they may volunteer. The key is for the assessor to be viewed as impartial, trustworthy, and capable.

   If the assessment is convened early, before hostilities arise and while the situation is relatively simple, the assessment may be easier to conduct. In these situations, the assessment may be completed informally, perhaps by community members or local leaders serving as the assessor. This can be done inexpensively and with administrative ease. In the Discordia case, for instance, the city planner might begin by informally reaching out to various parties to assess the situation and produce a brief report outlining the key concerns and process recommendations for moving forward. However, in complex or long-standing disputes where contentious relationships have developed and the facts are disputed, a professional mediator may be needed to serve as the assessor. In Discordia, the city planner feels comfortable serving as the assessor since the process has started early and the issues are not too complex.

Professional mediators are great assessors because they have expertise helping stakeholders separate positions from interests, protecting confidential statements, and synthesizing findings in a constructive way. Outside mediators should be used when the decision will have a high impact on stakeholders; the issues are complex; there are many parties; tensions are high and relationships frayed; previous efforts to address the conflict have failed; or funds are available to hire a mediator.

While assessors work closely with the conveners to design and carry out the assessment, they will—and should—remain independent and impartial regardless of the convener's point of view. The assessor must work on behalf of all the stakeholders and not as an advocate or consultant who is solely accountable to the convener. Doing otherwise would jeopardize the legitimacy of the assessment.

- *How Long Do Assessments Take, and How Much Do They Cost?* The duration and cost of assessments vary greatly. A quick assessment carried out by a community member may take a few weeks and cost nothing, while a complex assessment performed by an outside mediator may take a year or more and may cost tens of thousands of dollars. It takes time to develop an interview protocol, identify the list of interviewees, conduct the interviews, and analyze the data. A dispute between a neighborhood and a developer over an eight-unit condo development, for example, might be assessed in a few weeks. For a complex project involving tens of millions of dollars of investment, an assessment may take several months.
- *What Sources of Financial Support Are Available and Legitimate?* For conveners who do not have the funding to hire an assessor, assistance may be sought from foundations, academic institutions, government agencies, think tanks, stakeholders, or local businesses.

Government resources, funding from groups of stakeholders, or support from foundations and academic institutions are often well regarded. However, conveners should be mindful of how stakeholder groups will perceive all funding streams. If funding comes from the municipality or the developer, it is important that the source is not perceived all influencing the outcome. In general, there is no single approach to successfully fund an assessment, but it is our experience that citizens care about the source of funding. Methods to fund assessments must be transparent and acceptable to the participating groups.

### Step 2: Design the Assessment

Once an assessor is selected and the process has begun, one of the first tasks will be to design the assessment. This stage involves determining what topics are relevant and who should be interviewed. Making this determination involves conducting research and interviews to understand the nature of the decision.

- *Background Research.* Assessors research the history of the situation and the community by reviewing reports, news articles, and other sources. They work with the convener to identify the broad issues that need to be addressed in the assessment. In the Discordia case, because the town does not have the money to hire an assessor, the planner will play the role of the assessor. First, she must get a sense of the range of topics people are concerned about through newspapers, local press, or statements made by various groups. She may also begin to gather technical information that participants might use later in the process and will supplement this with additional information she gathers later during the interviews.
- *Choice of Interviewees.* The list of stakeholders to be interviewed should include those who

- are involved or see themselves as involved in the decision;
- are likely to offer new and different views of the decision;
- represent stakeholders who are reticent about being involved;
- are especially concerned about the decision;

- are necessary to implement an outcome (decision makers); and
- are likely to be impacted by the outcome.

Typical stakeholders fall into three categories: governmental (municipal, state, national, and quasi-governmental), private sector (landowners and other business owners), and nongovernmental organizations (local citizens' groups, citizen task forces, and environmental groups). Some of the specific interviewees include municipal staff, elected officials, regional or state-level staff, developers, conservation groups, economic development offices, adjacent landowners, neighborhood groups, technical experts, and community leaders.

The town planner in Discordia decides that the interviewees for the assessment should include the developer and representatives of the abutting property owners: the National Bank, the Petroil gas station, the Super-Mart, the Burns Medical Complex, Quimby Elementary School, and the Bailey Apartments. She recognizes that the elementary school and Bailey Apartments have a range of representatives. To understand all the interests represented by these groups, she will need to talk to different constituencies. At the school, she will talk with teachers, administrators, and parents. At the apartments, she will consult the management company, the owners, and the renters. Based on her background research, she will interview the local environmental group as well.

It is crucial that the interviewees include people who represent less visible and less organized constituencies. This might include seasonal visitors; individuals who are concerned about a site, but do not belong to a membership group; populations who are less likely to self-identify (often including minority groups, lower-income groups, the elderly, and the young); and individuals who are concerned, but do not trust the convener or assessor. In some cases, especially in communities with weak citizen participation in organized groups, the assessors may have to interview individual citizens rather than representatives of membership groups. James Kent Associates uses a discovery process in which citizens informally collect information at community gathering places (James Kent Associates 2012). They interview people on the street, in grocery stores, or on public transportation to hear the opinions of people who might never attend a public meeting on a community planning project issue.

- **Interview Protocol.** In addition to researching the background and identifying interviewees, the assessors must develop an interview protocol. The background information plays a central role in creating the interview protocol because the assessors will use the interviews to confirm what they know, identify information that might not have been revealed, and uncover stakeholder priorities. The interview questions are open ended and designed to uncover the stakeholders' varied perspectives of the situation and recommendations on how to proceed.

---

**Box 4.3**

**Questions Interviewees Should Be Asked**

- What is their role and background in the situation?
- What is their perspective on the situation (their experience, how they feel about it, and what they hope for in the future)?
- What is their view on relevant politics and the history of the relationship among the players?
- Would a collaborative process make sense and, if so, under what conditions?
- Is there anything else the assessment team should know in order to have a complete picture of the situation? (This final question often generates valuable information.)

---

The interview protocol should also be designed to discover the participants' willingness to come to the deliberation table. How open to a participatory process are they? Under what conditions would they participate? When these questions are asked while interviewing stakeholders (Step 3), they help the assessors formulate the recommendations for designing the process (Step 6).

- **Additional Data Collection Methods.** In addition to interviews and document review, assessments can utilize different methods to collect data. Assessors can use email or anonymous Web surveys, which can provide important information while enabling a wide range of participants to contribute.

**Box 4.4**

**Online, Low-Cost Survey Tools**

- Use online tools such as Zoomerang or SurveyMonkey.
- Develop questions collaboratively with multiple stakeholders to ensure they are fair and balanced.
- Provide adequate time for responses.
- Broadcast the link widely.
- Organize and share the results while protecting confidentiality.

In Falmouth, Maine, in 2009, we assisted the town and a diverse stakeholder committee to reconsider Falmouth's overall planning process, subcommittees, and approach. As part of the assessment, a short online survey was developed. The town emailed the survey to its listserv of people interested in land use issues and posted it on the town's website. Surprisingly, though the questions were about the decision-making process and not about any particular project, a large number of citizens responded with input and advice.

- *Outreach.* Once the assessment has been designed, either the convener or the assessment team drafts an introductory letter or email to prospective interviewees to explain the assessment process and invite them to participate. The explanation in this letter, listing the names of the organizations leading the process, is important to legitimize the effort. The communication should indicate that the interviews are confidential, provide contact information to schedule interviews, and explain how the results will be used. Several days after the letter arrives, a follow-up phone call should be made to begin scheduling interviews. This initial contact is the first opportunity to articulate the intent, steps, and value of the assessment.

**Step 3: Interview Stakeholders**

After all the preparations are complete, the assessment interviews get under way. Interviews can take place in person or over the phone. In-person assessment interviews generally take 30 minutes to one hour. The more controversial the decision, the more beneficial it is to interview in person. This builds relationships and trust. The assessor may decide to set up in a particular central location (for example, a room in a public building or café) or may meet interviewees in the location of their choosing. The town planner, concerned about the acrimony that the mall redevelopment issue is raising in Discordia, decides to interview the stakeholders in person on their turf. This communicates a good faith effort to work with them.

Confidentiality is paramount; individuals will not be quoted or have particular statements attributed to them. Generally, only one member of an assessment team is present at each interview, though a second member of the team may attend as an observer or a note taker. The notes from the interviews are shared only within the assessment team, not with the convener, to encourage participants to speak freely.

The assessment is designed to capture a range of views without focusing on the particular individuals who share those views. On some occasions, the assessor will conduct a group interview instead of interviewing a representative. Small group interviews can be a cost-effective way to hear diverse perspectives and can help shy people to speak up if they are with a group of trusted peers. However, some people are likely not to speak quite as freely in a group as by themselves, so the assessment team should consider carefully whether to offer group interviews. Interviews are not normally recorded, as audio recording can make interviewees overly cautious about what they share and how it will be utilized. Instead, interviewers take written notes.

After completing the first interviews, the assessment team may fine-tune the protocol depending on how the first round was received. If the initial protocols seemed too detailed, or they made assumptions that were not appropriate or did not motivate participants to provide useful information, the assessment team will need to make modifications. Once the assessment team stops hearing new information in the interviews, they have interviewed enough stakeholders to understand the range of perspectives.

**Tips for Conducting Successful Assessment Interviews**

- Prepare open-ended questions in advance.
- Explain your role in the process.
- Ensure confidentiality.
- Ask probing follow-up questions.
- Listen and maintain an open mind.
- Take detailed notes, especially on underlying interests.
- Always ask "Is there anything else I should know?"

## Step 4: Analyze and Present the Findings

Once the interviews have been completed, the assessment team analyzes the responses and compiles their findings in a way that can be shared. The results of an assessment may be presented as a written report, as an executive summary, or even as a set of presentation slides with key points to help the stakeholders focus on the next steps. The report describes the decision that has to be made, presents the most important issues as identified by the stakeholders, and offers some suggestions about what type of mutual gains process (if any) might make sense going forward.

In the Discordia case, in her role as the assessor, the town planner does not have the time or resources to generate a lengthy report. Instead, she prepares a brief memo that identifies the range of interests raised by the following issues: traffic patterns, noise, lighting, stream restoration, site contamination and cleanup, garbage storage and disposal, and building design.

She also offers options for how to proceed, which range from doing nothing beyond the existing administrative proceedings to setting up a series of strategic, multistakeholder group meetings. The city planner then sends the draft report to the interviewees for comment.

An assessment report typically contains a brief description of assessment methodology, including names of interviewees; the interview protocol (the list of questions asked); findings, which might include information on the historical, legal, or policy contexts; stakeholders' concerns and hopes; the economics of the project; environmental concerns; a list of key stakeholder groups; and recommendations for moving forward, which could range from recommending additional processes, such as meetings, to suggesting that the current circumstances are not right for productive collaboration.

The two key components of an assessment report are the findings section and the process recommendations. The findings should reflect the range of views shared by interviewees without attribution to capture both key points and the force of the sentiments accurately without advancing any particular perspective. The language used should not contribute to schisms between groups, but should state the facts as understood across the interviews. For example, the Discordia city planner writes in her findings: "Many felt that this project as currently designed would jeopardize the safety of the school children, while others felt that safety concerns were not an issue given actual traffic patterns." This approach describes a range of views without indicating bias or breaking confidentiality. Writing a findings section requires the ability to see the situation clearly and to accurately present the divergent voices. In presenting the findings, the assessment team may map overlapping and opposing interests and ideas, identify ideas that seemed to have traction across a range of groups, and highlight areas of significant disagreement or opposition. They will likely also be looking for barriers to reaching agreement down the road.

---

**Box 4.6**

**Questions an Assessment Should Answer**

- What are the key issues in this situation or conflict?
- What is the range of interests for each issue?
- Who has been involved and how?
- Is collaborative negotiation an option for resolving this situation?
- If so, how would the process be structured?
- What would a satisfactory outcome look like?
- What constraints apply (political, legal, timing, or resources)?

---

## Step 5: Decide Whether to Proceed

The next step is a crucial one. The assessment team recommends whether or not to proceed with a mutual gains effort. This decision should be based on the timing in relation to the required process, the affected parties, the issues for negotiation, and the process options. Too many difficulties in any of these areas may suggest that collaboration will be a challenge (see figure 4.1). Once the assessment team makes their recommendations, the stakeholders and convener must jointly decide whether and how to proceed. This is a combined decision between the stakeholders and the convener because commitment and resources are needed from both.

■ *Timing.* Although a given conflict may be appropriate for a mutual gains process, timing considerations may increase or decrease the likelihood of success. Not all entry points for collaboration are equally effective. In the beginning, the opportunity to reach agreement among the stakeholders is high. Stakeholders are able to consider a range of alternatives because they have not publicly committed to a detailed outcome. Yet, at this early stage, the project details are often unclear. Without a specific proposal to which individuals can react, without a dispute or threat to motivate and galvanize participation, it may be hard to get input. Therefore, in the early stages when there is the most opportunity to develop creative ideas, explore numerous options, and weave diverse interests together, there may be the least motivation for the stakeholders to engage in negotiation.

As a proposal moves through the process, the stakeholders become increasingly involved and committed to their positions. The applicant has now spent significant resources on site engineering, design, and financing consistent with a specific proposal. She may feel reluctant to consider major changes in the proposal. Likewise, citizens have also become committed to their positions through public statements or coalitions. Room for bargaining at this point may be more constrained than earlier. If the early opportunities have passed, the parties may have to spend time fighting it out. Thus, the assessor should be cognizant of timing when making recommendations.

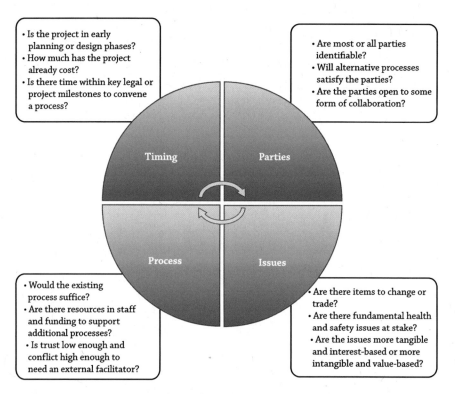

- Is the project in early planning or design phases?
- How much has the project already cost?
- Is there time within key legal or project milestones to convene a process?

- Are most or all parties identifiable?
- Will alternative processes satisfy the parties?
- Are the parties open to some form of collaboration?

Timing

Parties

Process

Issues

- Would the existing process suffice?
- Are there resources in staff and funding to support additional processes?
- Is trust low enough and conflict high enough to need an external facilitator?

- Are there items to change or trade?
- Are there fundamental health and safety issues at stake?
- Are the issues more tangible and interest-based or more intangible and value-based?

FIGURE 4.1 Factors to Consider in the Decision to Proceed Beyond the Assessment

After years of fighting, the stakeholders may once again be willing to negotiate. They are aware of the costs associated with a lack of agreement and the issues are more defined. Unfortunately, at this point, the parties are often even more committed to their positions (having expended extensive resources of time and money) and may find it difficult to create joint gains. Hence, the dilemma of timing: at the beginning of the process, stakeholders may not be motivated to negotiate, but there are more options for reaching an agreement. At the end of the process, stakeholders are motivated, but there are fewer options for reaching agreement.

There is no hard and fast rule about when in the required process a mutual gains approach is appropriate. Many disputes finally settle after years of repeated efforts at resolution because of new perspectives on the problem, new opportunities (a party to the dispute can finally afford to contribute financially), or new stakeholders (an entrenched player is replaced by his successor, who is more creative). This is what happened at Assembly Square in Somerville, Massachusetts. After almost a decade of fighting among the city, developers, and residents, a new mayor and a new set of development negotiators were able to reach an agreement with the residents. Alternately, when cases have not been settled, negotiation efforts may have already covered all of the possible offers and compromises, leaving little room left to negotiate.

As a general rule, land use decisions are well positioned for successful collaboration if the proposal is far enough along to be well described and understood by the public, but not so well developed that there is little opportunity for new ideas.

- **Parties.** First, there must be a way to identify and communicate with most of the individuals or groups who will be affected by the outcome of the decision. Second, the parties must have some interest in supplementing the required decision-making process. If parties feel that they can accomplish most of their objectives through the required process or in court, then there is little incentive for them to engage in a collaborative process. Finally, the parties must be willing to negotiate in good faith. If one of the central parties is ideologically opposed to negotiating with another, a mutual gains effort may not be successful.

- **Issues.** The issues or topics implicated in a land use decision can range from few to many. How large a store will be, the number of units, the type of signage, the extent of habitat preservation, or level of environmental mitigation are examples of issues. If one group is adamantly opposed to any form of development or ideologically opposed to the concept of comprehensive planning, reaching agreement on any of the substantive issues is unlikely.

- **Process.** Proceeding with a mutual gains effort involves evaluating the underlying decision and determining if supplementing that process is appropriate. Much of this subject was covered in chapters 2 and 3 through the exploration of the required decision-making process. If the underlying process will adequately meet the needs of the parties, then a supplemental collaborative process may not be appropriate. If, however, stakeholder needs are more likely to be satisfied through a mutual gains process, the next process question is: Are there resources to support it? Supplemental collaborative processes take time, money, and effort. If all stakeholders are not willing to commit appropriate levels of resources, then the process should not go forward. Finally, if resources are available, the stakeholders may want to consider employing a professional to help facilitate discussions and mediate negotiations.

In deciding whether the threshold for a collaborative process has been met, the assessor should carefully consider the situation and reflect on similar cases. The option not to proceed with a mutual gains effort must always remain on the table. If the recommendation is not to move forward, the assessments may have saved time, money, and effort by preventing a process that would have been unproductive.

Despite strong emotions and significant issues in Discordia, the town planner—as the assessor—senses that there may be opportunity for collaboration. The development has been specifically described and the developer is open to adjusting the plan to try to meet some of the abutters' concerns. Parents are very concerned and have threatened a lawsuit, but they are not particularly well organized or well funded. Although the town council might be sympathetic to neighborhood concerns, they have publicly stated that they want this parcel developed and that increasing the tax base is essential for keeping residential property tax rates manageable for most families. The assessor, with information from confidential conversations with many stakeholders, decides that there is potential for a mutual gains effort to go forward. She makes that recommendation to the stakeholders and the convener in person and in the assessment report.

## Step 6: Design the Process

If the assessor recommends a mutual gains process, that recommendation should specifically link process alternatives with interview findings. In the assessment report, the assessor should outline the purpose of the process, the issues to be covered, a draft of the ground rules, governing laws that must be followed, stakeholders to be included, an outline of the work plan, and an estimate of how long it will take. Often, this will include recommendations such as how many meetings to hold, how long the process should last, and how the public should be involved.

- ***Who Designs the Process?*** The reality of practice is that the detailed design of the process is completed in the stage between the assessment and the official launch of the collaboration, which is more thoroughly explored in chapter 5. Designing the process is complicated. Since many stakeholders want to have a voice in the design, issues of ownership, trust, and legitimacy often arise. While some group, organization, or individual will have served as convener, after the assessment team talks to a wide range of people, it is possible that the task of designing the process may be completed by others in addition to the convener.

## Step 7: Share the Results

The final step in an assessment is to share the results. An assessment report is typically shared in draft form with the interviewees, either with or without the recommendations section. Interviewees then have the opportunity to note if information is missing or needs reframing. This step increases the accuracy of the document, builds trust, and ensures that the report reflects the perspective of the stakeholders. While assessment reports can highlight differences in opinion, they often reveal the commonalities among different people, including those across stakeholder groups.

Once final feedback from interviewees is obtained and the document is revised, the report, including findings, recommendations, list of interviewees, and interview protocol, is finalized and made public.

Assessments give those who want to improve a decision-making process the information to determine a range of appropriate processes. An assessment report describes the issues, context, background, process options, and challenges. Through interviews and meetings, thoughtfully executed assessments provide the foundation for effective engagement with all stakeholders. The focus may then move from identifying the issue of concern to designing a collaborative process appropriate for that development decision. The next chapter considers how to design processes for collaborative engagement in difficult land use disputes.

# CHAPTER 5

■ ■ ■ ■ ■ □ □ □ □

# Designing a Process for Collaboration

## WHAT IS PROCESS DESIGN?

Process design is the deliberate effort of the participants to identify the key elements of a process. It is the game plan for a series of meetings. Planning how to engage people effectively is often based on the data and information collected in the assessment, as described in the previous chapter. Some assessments only describe the parties, issues, and concerns in a given situation. Other assessments recommend, in general or in detail, the key elements of process design for the effort to move forward. This chapter describes how to design an effective, collaborative process, as part of the recommendations included in an assessment or separately.

When a local community faces a difficult situation, it is common for the decision makers (mayor, town council, or others) to refer the problem to a committee without conducting an assessment. This can be either an existing committee, which may not be functioning well, or a newly created, ad hoc, situation-specific committee. The committee might be representative of the range of interested stakeholders, the city's opinion leaders, or the friends of those in power. In any case, the committee is given a task and a deadline. The elected officials then breathe a temporary sigh of relief, hoping that the committee will resolve the difficult conflict with a final decision that is not too costly politically.

When these committees fail, it is often for one or more of the following reasons.

■ The scope of their activities was not carefully considered.
■ The selected participants did not represent the range of interests.

- The connections between the committee, the public, and political authority were not well established.
- The timeline was too long or too short.
- The committee was underresourced.

Good process design begins with good process infrastructure. You cannot build a thriving city without the necessary infrastructure (water, streets, sewers, and open space) and you cannot create durable, widely supported decisions without sufficient process infrastructure (assessment, design, deliberation, and implementation). If assessment is likened to surveying, site investigation, and legal due diligence, process design is the act of designing and engineering the process within which the community works. Though there is no guarantee of success, good process design will increase the likelihood of broad agreement among stakeholders.

Discordia's town planner, who performed the role of assessor, is now taking on the role of facilitator. She asks a number of the assessment interviewees to serve on a committee that will generate and evaluate options for the old mall site. She is not sure exactly how the committee will work or who will be on it, but she is initiating conversations with the stakeholders about how they envision the process would be designed.

Some of the initial questions in process design, such as who should convene and pay for the process, are covered in chapter 4 on assessment. This chapter introduces additional questions that must be asked when designing a mutual gains process.

---

**Box 5.1**

### Questions to Ask When Designing a Mutual Gains Process

- What is the intent of the process?
- Which issues will be addressed?
- Who will determine which issues will be addressed?
- Who will manage the process?
- What is the schedule for the process?
- What is the product of the process?
- How does the stage of the decision shape the design of the process?

---

- How can the process be designed to make municipal approval more likely?
- How can appropriate stakeholder groups be built?
- What can be done to ensure the public at large is included?
- What is the role of technical experts?
- Why should independent experts be hired?
- Why should an expert be selected jointly?
- How can technical knowledge be developed collaboratively?

## WHAT IS THE INTENT OF THE PROCESS?

Defining the intent of the process is an essential, early decision. Is the purpose simply to *inform* stakeholders about a project? Is the intent to *gather advice* on a project? Is the intent to *engage* the stakeholders in generating acceptable options? Or, is the intent to work out a solution, to *decide* together? The conveners of a process must be crystal clear about their intent for a process in order to prevent conflict with stakeholders' expectations.

A range of groups including the International Association for Public Participation (IAP2) and the U.S. Environmental Protection Agency have developed frameworks to assist conveners and stakeholders to think systematically about their intent when initiating a collaborative, public process. If the intent is to explore and inform the public about the issues, the convener must be clear that the process is not a negotiation or an opportunity to significantly modify the developer's plans based on public input. Many federal agencies are required under the National Environmental Policy Act (NEPA) to collect information from stakeholders. The public is informed of the issues, the alternatives, and the draft recommendations, and can comment in writing and at a single public hearing. But NEPA does not require the agencies to change their decisions based on these comments. Three common purposes of public processes include informing, advising, and decision making.

- **Informing** involves letting the stakeholders know about a proposal, a set of options, or a general plan. It does not imply that the decision maker is seeking stakeholder advice or recommendations, or is sharing any decision-making authority.

- *Advising* implies that a convener is seeking recommendations that are specific and actionable. Again, seeking advice does not imply that the decision maker will necessarily act on the comments provided or share any of their decision-making authority.
- *Decision making* is the least frequent and most difficult intent to accomplish. It implies that stakeholders have the right to a very active part in deliberations, but also implies that they have the responsibility to work diligently and actively toward an agreement or settlement.

The collaborative processes described in this book go beyond informing the stakeholders to engaging them in decision making.

## WHICH ISSUES WILL BE ADDRESSED?

The scope of the deliberations must be determined. In many cases, the key issues for deliberation may be well known and widely supported. However, this is not often the case with significant development decisions. First, complex and somewhat unbounded issues, such as a master plan for the next 10 years, may make it difficult for the parties to determine what is or is not on the table: environmental protection, climate change, population growth, economic growth (or lack thereof), jobs, or transportation. For example, climate change as a planning issue may seem to have a daunting scope since climate change may involve sea level rise, changes in precipitation and storm water, heat waves, and so forth, causing impacts on public health, land use, property values, public infrastructure, and more.

Ideally, for complex issues in which the scope may be in dispute, two important steps should be taken. First, the convener should establish broad goals for the process to provide a sense of general boundaries. For instance, when dealing with a transportation issue, goals might be to reduce traffic congestion, increase public safety, and engage stakeholders in the decision. Second, the convener should treat the scoping of issues as a deliberative process so stakeholders can shape the debate. For example, stakeholders might work with the convener to define which issues will be the subject of the negotiations.

A typical, environmental impact statement (EIS) process begins with a scoping meeting to identify the issues to be studied. Some scoping processes allow the public to identify any issue they believe relevant to the project. The federal agency then determines which of the issues are relevant enough to include in the EIS and which are not, but the process at least starts in this broad way. The positive result of this exercise is to allow the public to name the issues. However, such scoping meetings also tend to generate a wide array of issues and ultimately leave the decision about what to include up to the federal agency. In this case, some stakeholders do not have input in the topic selection, may not understand why their issue was left out, and may feel marginalized or ignored.

## WHO WILL DETERMINE WHICH ISSUES WILL BE ADDRESSED?

In the Assembly Square case, during the assessment conducted many years into the development process, the developers felt tremendous time pressure due to financial commitments and they wanted a resolution as soon as possible. The developers insisted that the one key component not up for negotiation was ownership of the properties. The development site had multiple owners and two primary developers. During the assessment, it became clear that the parcel slated for commercial development was actually better suited to residential development. Ultimately, the final agreement that resolved most issues involved a property swap. By adopting a shorter-sighted view of the problem and refusing to discuss ownership, a key stakeholder had prevented further dialogue on this linchpin issue. Interestingly, many negotiations are finally settled not because the parties narrowed the issues to the few they could agree upon, but rather because they added issues to the point where they could trade across issues in order to make a deal.

In complex decisions, it is essential that the convener and stakeholders wrestle with the issue of scope. They will need to ask many questions to help determine the scope. What do we want to do together that we cannot do as well apart? What topics are clearly connected to the key issue or questions? What is our capacity (financial, technical, and schedule) to tackle this subject? How many issues will we be able to work through, and at what level of depth and detail? What issues might be important pieces of the puzzle for packaging a successful approach?

A facilitator can help parties find ways to reframe the problem by adding or removing issues, which increases the chances of reaching agreement.

## WHO WILL MANAGE THE PROCESS?

In most public meetings, workshops, and group events, someone has to manage the process. In traditional settings with committees, councils, and other formal bodies, a chair usually runs meetings according to *Robert's Rules of Order*—the popular manual describing how motions are made and voting procedures are established. This standard practice is tried and true for formal settings (though see Susskind and Cruikshank's *Breaking Robert's Rules* [2006] for an alternative approach even in these settings), but for collaborative processes, such a formal structure tends to be counterproductive. Chairs are often also decision makers who may steer meetings and manage complex parliamentary rules to ensure a particular outcome. Effective collaboration needs more than just a chair to effectively manage the process. A facilitator or mediator may be needed to manage the complexity of a significant development decision.

Ideally, a neutral professional will be hired to manage the design process. If professional mediation is not available or affordable, other options include retired or former officials who may have the trust and stature among stakeholders. State or federal agencies may have staff trained in mediation who are knowledgeable about land use issues. Sometimes local dispute resolution organizations, such as community mediation centers, can provide affordable mediation services.

Facilitators may be found in a variety of places. Boston's Metropolitan Area Planning Council wanted its staff to be most visible in the public process when it undertook the MetroSolutions project. The council hired a facilitation firm to help design the process and train its staff as the process unfolded. The City of Albuquerque, New Mexico, keeps on hand a roster of local facilitators and, through a modest budget, provides facilitation from an independent professional for some meetings in controversial cases. For Albuquerque's North 4th Street Corridor case from 2007 to 2008, the city and its stakeholders retained the services of a college planning professor and a highly skilled facilitator.

A gravel pit expansion in East Middlebury, Vermont, is an interesting example of creative facilitator selection (Nolon 2012). Susan Shashok, a concerned resident, decided something needed to be done to help resolve the conflict, and she stepped in as an informal convener and facilitator. Susan put in over 800 volunteer hours during the process. She felt that she was right for the job of leading the process because she had a flexible schedule as a stay-at-home mom, had time to devote to the project, missed her professional work, and had experience as a manager. She was also committed to, and curious about, the issues and was optimistic about the potential for effective collaboration. While this is an unusual case, it shows that a competent and trusted facilitator may play a variety of roles and may be found in a variety of associations and walks of life.

---

**Box 5.2**

**Tips for Selecting the Right Facilitator or Mediator**

A mediator's technical and institutional background should be closely matched to the situation and the stakeholders. Participants react to style and personal chemistry. Typical criteria for selecting a facilitator include:

- level of experience; years of casework; number of similar disputes handled successfully; substantive/technical knowledge; training; style (active or passive style, tone, level of forcefulness); reputation in the field; professional affiliations; references; and personality.

---

## WHAT IS THE SCHEDULE FOR THE PROCESS?

Each process will have its own schedule requirements. A comprehensive planning process may be driven by state requirements to update a plan at prescribed intervals. In a court-related case, there may be clear deadlines that require the parties to resolve issues within a predetermined time frame.

Scheduling the length and timing of a process can be one of the trickier components of process design because stakeholders' incentives may not be aligned. For example, parties often value time differently. In general, a developer is faced with the very real pressures of financing; the cost of loans is directly tied to the length of development and to general and dynamic market conditions. The sooner a developer can construct the project and begin generating cash flow, the better for its bottom line. Neighboring abutters worry about the long-term impacts of traffic, noise, and shadows on their neighborhood and care about getting the project right, rather than getting the project done. They may be willing to spend months or years thinking through what outcome would be best. Depending on the extent of the issues, some parties may want to know much more before making a decision, while others may have a higher risk tolerance and be willing to make decisions in the face of uncertainty. Elected officials may also face time pressures to show results before the next election or else be faced with town finance concerns, which can mean that a decision today, however suboptimal in the future, is better for them than no decision at all.

These complexities can make it difficult to create a timeline that satisfies everyone. Too short a deadline usually means the discussion and process are truncated. When a time frame is too long, the participants become worn out, and the demographics and economics can change enough during this lapse that the parties need to revisit seemingly settled issues. In addition, time pressures can help bring parties to the table and focus on the task at hand.

The convener must balance these considerations and her own interests regarding the timeline and schedule. It is better for the convener to decide on a timeline together with stakeholders than to act unilaterally. Working with stakeholders on this can simply mean giving them a draft timeline and asking for advice, or it can mean actually negotiating the process schedule intensively for larger, longer-term projects.

## WHAT IS THE PRODUCT OF THE PROCESS?

A mutual gains process usually results in more than conversation, increased understanding, better relationships, and meeting agendas and summaries. For advisory and decision-making processes, the goal is usually a final report, recommendations, or a plan that will lead to a decision. Thus, from the beginning, conveners should be clear about what product they would like produced at the end of the process. The participants in the process should help shape not only the content, but also the form of such a product.

In some cases, the product may be a set of broad recommendations or principles. Part of the final product in the Durham, New Hampshire, Mill Plaza process was a set of seven principles to guide redevelopment of the site. In the case of the MaxPak process (see table 1.2), the final product was a set of development guidelines for the neighborhood, along with the information and technical advice summarized in writing. In some cases, the final product is as specific as a master plan or a site plan. Final products are essential for capturing agreements in writing for the understanding of participants and those who will later implement them. They also help focus participants toward a common end.

## HOW DOES THE STAGE OF THE DECISION SHAPE THE DESIGN OF THE PROCESS?

The stage of the land use planning effort dictates at least some aspects of the process, as discussed in chapter 4. For instance, if the challenge is how best to engage the community in developing a comprehensive 10-year plan, the process will differ from a site-specific development project that raises a discrete set of contentious issues. It is likely that a comprehensive planning effort would not be as contentious as the site-specific development project because the stakeholders are discussing visions for the general community rather than deciding what will be built on a known parcel. However, in some communities, any land use decision causes controversy.

## HOW CAN A PROCESS BE DESIGNED TO MAKE MUNICIPAL APPROVAL MORE LIKELY?

Understanding how the mutual gains approach fits within the required decision-making process is essential to its success. In the 1970s, during a period of increasing use of collaborative processes in land use planning, well-intended citizens sometimes banded together in the spirit of good and open government to wrestle with local land use comprehensive plans or other issues. After months of hard work, they brought their recommendations before the elected officials. The elected officials often responded negatively because they neither sanctioned nor participated in the process.

Frustrated citizens would then become angry, and elected officials might even reassert their authority, for better or worse.

To determine how the supplemental process fits with the required process, the convener can ensure that some decision makers are either active participants or active liaisons in the process. For instance, local, elected officials can be asked to serve as members of a process design committee. In many cases a staff person for the town can participate on behalf of the decision-making board. In the Chelsea Salt Dock case (see table 1.2), committee members included the city manager who, though not the ultimate decision maker, had strong and direct ties to the city's elected officials. In some cases, local or state law may discourage members of the decision-making boards from participating as members of ad hoc committees. Nonetheless, most jurisdictions allow at least one official board member on the committee in an advisory capacity. In the Somerville Assembly Square assessment process, a city councillor played just such an advisory role, but engaged actively to ensure close coordination among the required and informal processes (see chapter 3).

## HOW CAN APPROPRIATE STAKEHOLDER GROUPS BE BUILT?

One of the challenges of land use planning is that the number of affected parties can be quite large. In Albuquerque's North 4th Street Corridor case, potential stakeholders included the many large and small businesses along the corridor, residents on or near the corridor, various associations representing some of these parties, drivers, patrons of the businesses, the city's bus system, the city government, state agencies that fund transportation projects, and public health groups.

As chapter 4 explains, a key stage of assessment and process design is to identify all the possible stakeholders, identify groups or organizations that represent those stakeholders, and find individuals or representatives who can speak with some legitimacy and authority on behalf of those stakeholders. If an assessment has been done prior to process design, the parties to be involved will already be identified. If the process does not include the time or budget for a full assessment, at the very least the conveners must develop a list of potential stakeholders, organizations, and individuals who should be included.

If a key party is left out of early proceedings, the convener and the parties must decide whether and how to include it in the future. The Chelsea Salt Dock case is an example of an administrative proceeding that had to backtrack in order to include key missing stakeholders, the neighborhood and its advocate, Chelsea Green Space. In master planning processes, the parties are, in a sense, every resident of the community, every business, and anyone who uses or visits the built and natural environment within that jurisdiction. This makes the task of deciding who should participate very difficult.

First, collaborative processes should be inclusive of the full range of interests affected by the decision. Most local and state laws require that decisions be made in public view. To avoid angry or marginalized stakeholders, both for the sake of fairness and to avoid opposition to decisions after they have been made, more rather than fewer stakeholders should be included. While adding more stakeholders can be time consuming and increase the complexity of the process (from finding common ground to simply scheduling meetings), these stakeholders can bring interests, perspectives, and options to the table that otherwise might not be included and can help ensure that the final product or agreement is legitimate and credible.

Second, any process should achieve some level of balance across groups. One set of stakeholders may be particularly motivated to participate because they feel directly affected and may wish to have multiple representatives participate in negotiations. Other affected parties may be harder to identify and organize. In addition, balanced groups do not exclude angry or upset stakeholder groups, but rather include them along with many other stakeholders. Balance helps produce good public policy by seeking input from a diversity of affected stakeholders and ensuring that different voices are heard.

Third, the participant group has to be manageable and practical in size. While it is possible to seek advice from hundreds of people, decision-making processes almost always require a limited number of people, representing larger constituencies, who can work through issues, invent options, and wrestle collectively with difficult trade-offs. Although decision-making processes may include groups as large as 60 or 70, groups this large require substantial levels of management, facilitation, logistics, and time. More typically, agreement-building processes include anywhere from 10 to 20 core participants, with supplemental ways for many others to participate, such as public comment periods, committee meetings coupled with public workshops, interactive websites, and the use of social media.

Fourth, regardless of the ultimate makeup of a committee or group, the process and criteria for selecting representative members must be *transparent, clear, and public*. Ideally, the stakeholder groups have been identified through the conflict assessment, and it has been determined, perhaps through review of the assessment's findings, that no perspectives have been inadvertently omitted. Stakeholders might self-select and choose a representative, or a city manager or committee might ask for nominations within those categories. Then, according to publicly available criteria, the final representatives will be selected.

Last, it is important that the process helps ensure that representatives are *legitimate*. Legitimacy has several aspects. The constituency must confirm that the representative is a reasonable proxy or agent for its interests. For example, an elected president of a local neighborhood association who has clear responsibilities would be a likely candidate. It can be more difficult to identify legitimate representatives of loosely organized interests. For instance, in a local recreational conflict surrounding a town park, it may be hard to find an organized group that represents walkers, dog owners, or skate boarders. Yet these are legitimate interests that should be heard. In these cases, the convener may help stakeholders organize themselves for the process or provide a forum for participation in which anyone is welcome at any meeting.

Criteria for selecting legitimate representatives should ensure that the candidate represents an organized group and is sanctioned by that group in writing; is able to make commitments on behalf of the organization; is willing to follow the ground rules and scope outlined in the assessment; has the necessary time for the process; and is willing to work with others.

The following examples illustrate the flexibility required of the convener to create an appropriate process in structuring representation. In the North 4th Street case, subsequent to the assessment, residents and merchants each selected six representatives as well as six alternates to sit at the negotiating table. Previous efforts at appointing representatives had not succeeded, so self-selection among the identified stakeholder groups was essential. Two members of the planning staff, an agency director, and the staff planner in charge of the project participated in the negotiations as well. All meetings were open to the public, and the representatives were charged with ensuring their constituencies understood and could contribute to the process. Ground rules for communication and collaboration were established during the group's initial meetings.

In the Meriden, Connecticut, downtown planning process from 2004 to 2005, it became clear in the early stage of planning that key minority and affordable housing groups had previously been left out, as in the early stage of the North 4th Street Corridor case. The Meriden assessment identified 20 stakeholder groups that should be represented on the advisory group to ensure that a broad range of viewpoints would be shared. The assessment stressed that the group's meetings should be open to the public, with broad outreach and advertising. These 20 groups were asked to select representatives for the committee.

Interestingly, despite the long-standing, public fight over the site's future, the final process in the Assembly Square case included only the citizens group (Mystic View Task Force), the developers, and the mediators. The city's representatives decided against participating so they would not impose their influence and would give the key disputants the space to come to an agreement.

---

**Box 5.3**

### Tips for Building an Appropriate Stakeholder Group

- Determine a fair, open, and transparent method to select participants.
- Determine the appropriate number of representatives in total and per stakeholder group to form the committee.
- Brainstorm with the broad interest groups, such as the developer, abutters, land conservation groups, and local businesses.
- Consider as many organizations as possible in each interest area, at the local, state, and national levels.
- Identify individuals within each group or with each perspective who might participate.

## WHAT CAN BE DONE TO ENSURE THE
## PUBLIC AT LARGE IS INCLUDED?

Many processes are more informal than the structured and highly organized committees described here. They may include representative groups
and provide for general public participation. While broad public engagement is valuable, important, and often necessary, involving many people
in a meaningful way can also be difficult. Problems include inconsistent
participation, an individual versus constituency focus, incomplete understanding of issues, and lack of civility.

---

**Box 5.4**

**Methods to Involve the Public**

- Convene ongoing groups or committees (to get consistent participation and intense commitment) and open forums for all interested parties (for shared understanding and exchange).
- Provide timely, written information such as fact sheets, posters,
  maps, and information on websites and town bulletin boards.
- Provide multiple forums for participation, including poster
  sessions, workshops, and public meetings.
- Utilize webinars and conference calls, and tools such as online
  surveys, interactive websites, and social media.

---

First, a group needs time for education, understanding, building (or
rebuilding) trust, and identifying evaluating options. Even though it is
best to have a consistent set of participants, they do not always regularly
attend such meetings, which creates the need to review past meetings and
can result in frustration and slowed progress.

Second, because individual members of the public represent particular
viewpoints rather than a broader, organized constituency, they have little
incentive to offer shared views, build a consensus with other stakeholder
groups, or consider the needs of others.

Third, it can be difficult to ensure that a range of voices is heard. The
most organized and forceful groups will have the largest representation at
the meetings. This does not lead to the most stable outcomes. A decision

that strongly favors one set of stakeholders is likely to bring out another set ready to fight and sue, if necessary.

Fourth, generally those who are the loudest, angriest, and most difficult command the most attention and time of decision makers. Raucous town meetings and angry public hearings get media attention, but rarely tease out interests, reveal the range of views, and provide participants with the time and structure to carefully weigh the choices against long-term impacts.

While these challenges are substantial, there are ways to address them through collaborative processes. In the Wind Turbine Farm case in Manchester, Vermont, from 2005 to 2006, the coordinating team was small and structured, composed of town and village officials and the Orton Foundation. However, the process was conducted with the support and active participation of the planning board. The board hosted meetings on various technical topics and provided for extensive public comment and two public workshops in which any town or village resident, taxpayer, or business was encouraged to participate.

In the MaxPak case, the city of Somerville intentionally chose to engage anyone who wanted to join the effort rather than form a small committee during the initial part of the process. The goal was to bring together as many of the interested parties as possible to better understand their views and concerns, to educate them on a variety of aspects of development, and to encourage participants to discuss their differing views among themselves. The meetings were public, open to anyone interested, and each drew 50 to 60 participants representing a wide range of perspectives. Only after the broad public process in which participants agreed to develop neighborhood design guidelines did the city work with all participants to identify a subset of parties to work on the details of these guidelines.

The managers of most effective processes include ways to create smaller, focused groups of stakeholders that can connect in broader public engagement. In the Mill Plaza case in Durham, New Hampshire, from 2006 to 2008, the committee worked closely with consultants, developed key goals and principles, and deliberated on multiple issues. This committee held all of its meetings in public and taped each meeting to broadcast on public access television. The committee also recognized the fact that any plan would need broad support to have political merit, so the committee hosted a series of public meetings on scoping, design, and site planning, and allowed intensive interaction between the public and the design consultants.

Over the last 20 years, very sophisticated (albeit sometimes expensive) means for engaging the general public in more deliberative, representative forums have been developed. These tools include citizen juries and deliberative polling as well as those used by America*Speaks* such as keypad polling and "town hall" meetings. America*Speaks* uses various techniques to support large-scale public events, as they did to provide early input on the design of the former World Trade Center site after 9/11. America-*Speaks* conducts extensive public outreach, provides for as many as one thousand participants, uses numerous volunteer and paid staff to facilitate roundtable discussions, presents highly sophisticated graphics and presentations, and uses keypad polling to elicit nuanced opinions from participants on the issues at hand.

The Threshold Process case in San Mateo County in 2008 is an example of combining a variety of new tools to engage the broader public. The process was intended to focus regional attention on the problems of affordable housing, beyond any one municipality. The Threshold 2008 process ensured that a wide range of parties could participate through websites and public workshops. But it also ensured that leaders were able to get a clearer and more accurate sense of public sentiment by undertaking deliberative polling. Deliberative polling is a formalized method in which a diverse and randomly selected group of one hundred or more participants are invited to engage in an intensive, two-day process. Typically, prior to the two-day event, a smaller group of diverse stakeholders prepares a balanced, but detailed briefing book on the issues. In the two-day process, participants hear from a range of speakers on the issue (often of opposing views), ask questions, deliberate in small groups, and at the end of the process, complete a final survey. The results of this survey, completed by now-informed respondents, are then shared with the media, decision makers, and the public as representative of what the public thinks about an issue.

## WHAT IS THE ROLE OF
## TECHNICAL EXPERTS?

Land use decision making usually involves a number of technical considerations and the inherent uncertainty of planning for the future. Stakeholders in a development may care about future impacts such as noise, light,
odor, aesthetics, traffic, storm water, effects on existing businesses, and
future economic growth and taxes. Thus, they may need the services of
multiple technical experts to answer their questions. Good process design
anticipates the technical needs of a project and considers ways to integrate
that information into the decision-making process. The type of technical
experts needed should be based on the issues identified in the assessment.

According to David Cash and William Clark, there are three principles
to follow when looking for good technical support (Cash and Clark 2001).

- **Relevance**. Will the information meaningfully inform and be pertinent
  to the decision at hand?
- **Credibility**. Is the information viewed as defensible and of quality by
  other professionals?
- **Legitimacy**. Is the information believed by a diverse range of
  stakeholders?

What do these three principles mean? First, wetlands delineation might be
needed to determine whether a proposed development falls within a
wetland. However, if most stakeholders are worried about traffic and scale,
wetlands expertise may not be relevant to them. Second, the people
collecting, analyzing, and presenting information need to be credible in
the eyes of their professional peers. For instance, in a contentious land use
case, there can be painful moments when heated debate uncovers that the
basic inputs to a traffic model are wrong or that the air quality expert is
not knowledgeable. Professional competence is essential for technical
information to be considered seriously. Third, and perhaps most difficult,
is the notion of legitimacy. Even if the experts' information is relevant to a
case or if the experts are credible in the eyes of their professional peers, if
a set of stakeholders do not view the experts as legitimate, they will be
challenged and even disregarded. The legitimacy criterion can be hardest
to meet particularly if stakeholders are suspicious because the experts

were chosen and paid for by local government or the developer. To address this concern, developers have used creative arrangements to bring stakeholders into the process of selecting the experts. Various funding streams and arrangements between experts and stakeholders can be developed to meet these three principles.

## WHY SHOULD INDEPENDENT EXPERTS BE HIRED?

In the MaxPak case in Somerville, Massachusetts, city staff recognized that the stakeholders would need capable analyses of design, traffic, and the economics of the site, and that the developer's consultants would not be trusted given the public outcry about the large scale of the development. The city did not have the funds, expertise, or authority to design the project for the developer, so it asked the developer to provide modest funds to the city to contract independent experts to answer questions raised during the public process. The city then retained capable consultants who agreed not to work on the site going forward and who did not have existing or past relationships with the developer. The city hired an architect to discuss the site, including massing, scale, and interconnections to the existing neighborhood. The city also retained a traffic engineer to provide a basic analysis of existing data and to talk about different scales of development and potential traffic impacts. Last, the city brought in a professional real estate firm to explain the basic economics of the site and related implications for the types of units (studio, two bedroom, etc.), size of units (square footage per unit), and quality of units (amenities, quality of finish, etc.) related to the current and expected real estate market. As part of the process, these experts made initial presentations at public workshops, conducted modest analysis (the budget was limited) based on the public's interests, and returned to share and discuss that analysis.

This case reveals three valuable lessons about hiring experts. First, separate the funding for the process—including technical experts—from funding for the project. Second, use technical expertise to educate and enhance joint learning among stakeholders. Third, utilize independent technical experts distinct from the applicant's advisers to provide additional outside and trusted information.

## WHY SHOULD AN EXPERT BE
## SELECTED JOINTLY?

An effective way to hire an expert is to set up a joint decision-making process for hiring. When Boston sought a redesign of the Charles River Crossing as part of the Big Dig project, it confronted a legitimacy problem with what would eventually become the Leonard P. Zakim Bunker Hill Memorial Bridge. Many stakeholders had lost trust in the traffic engineers and bridge designers who had previously proposed convoluted and un-workable schemes, such as "Scheme Z," to move traffic over the Charles River from Boston to Cambridge.

When no design proved acceptable, a mediated process was used to find a better solution. Three subcommittees were created (traffic and transportation, open space, and visual design) in order to dissect the complex issues; develop shared, objective information; and brainstorm new bridge design options. The visual design committee requested and received unique authority to identify five independent experts who would

**Leonard P. Zakim Bunker Hill Memorial Bridge (2008).**
Source: iStockphoto/Denis Tangney, Jr.

be directly accountable to the committee—not to the decision-making agency. The committee selected as its independent bridge expert Christian Menn, a world-renowned bridge designer from Switzerland. It was he who, in interacting with the diverse stakeholder committee, finally arrived at the technically feasible, attractive design that was built. This structure is now a landmark for the city of Boston. Unlike the MaxPak case, in this instance, the committee selected their experts themselves. In the MaxPak case, there was neither the time nor the budget to jointly select technical assistance. However, as the Zakim Bridge case illustrates, for larger cases in which agency consultants may have lost credibility, joint selection of technical assistance can be an essential step in rebuilding trust.

## HOW CAN TECHNICAL KNOWLEDGE BE DEVELOPED COLLABORATIVELY?

A design charrette can be a very effective method for integrating technical resources into a collaborative process. In the 1990s, for instance, commercial development threatened the quiet commuter identity of the small city of Hercules in the San Francisco Bay area. Land values were increasing and plans for commercial and residential development were again being discussed after several years of recession. By the late 1990s, there were several controversial development proposals for a key site in the town.

The Hercules Planning Commission and City Council, with funds pooled from the Hercules Redevelopment Agency, landowners, and developers, initiated a charrette process. The 10-day charrette began on June 19, 2000, with public presentations. Design consultants provided information on transportation, housing, retail, and civil engineering. The plan produced during this intensive charrette was intended to provide a greater level of assurance to developers, landowners, and neighbors that the center of Hercules would be constructed in a manner aligned with the public's desires, namely, increased walkability, an appropriate amount of wild land preservation (there were some wetlands on the site), and a greater mix of uses. The joint funding of the experts, along with their skill in interacting with the public, gave them the credibility they needed.

# KEY LESSONS FOR GOOD PROCESS DESIGN

Lessons can be learned through studying the range of collaborative land use processes across the country. Concepts gathered from those examples follow.

- **Design the process with, not for, people.** A key element of successful process design is for conveners to work with the stakeholders in ways that allow the process itself, not just the substance, to be influenced and shaped by the stakeholders. This includes which issues are discussed, who participates in the process, and which experts are selected to support the dialogue.
- **Undertake an assessment.** Good process design should be based on past experience, professional skill, and good judgment, but also on the context-specific information about the situation. An effective assessment is the best tool for gathering and analyzing data and testing conclusions. Although many processes are designed without assessments, they increase the chances for better process design and success.
- **Select participants carefully.** Thoughtful consideration of participation will increase the likelihood of a successful process. Too often, participation is assigned to existing, organized stakeholders or selected based on political connections and past participation. This narrow approach to involvement can later undermine the perceived legitimacy of the process.
- **Link collaborative processes explicitly to formal decision making.** Collaborative, ad hoc processes can generate good ideas and goodwill. But a lack of clear connection to the decision makers and processes that have the authority to accept or deny action may result in frustration, further conflict, and inaction.
- **Provide multiple forms of participation to ensure full engagement.** Often, the public and stakeholders want to participate several ways, given the varied levels of interest and commitment. Thus, providing multiple means to participate ranging from a basic website to a year-long deliberative committee can engage most interests, gather ideas and concerns, and bring diverse views into decision making.
- **Ensure that technical support is professional, credible, and publicly legitimate.** Collaborative processes usually need technical support.

Such technical support is only effective if the experts are considered fair, capable, and independent by the stakeholders.

- **Set specific time frames and deliverables.** Collaborative processes, like all good projects, need clear scopes, time frames, and expected products or deliverables. Processes that are poorly planned frustrate participants and reduce the impact of their results. Schedules keep people on track, on budget, and moving toward common goals.

# CHAPTER 6

■ ■ ■ ■ ■ ■ □ □ □

# Facilitating Deliberations

After the assessment and the process design are completed, the planner from Discordia takes on the role of facilitator. She organizes a committee of interested stakeholders to work with the developer on generating and evaluating redevelopment options for the site. The committee includes representatives from adjacent schools and apartments, the environmental group working to protect the stream, and members of the historical society, among others. The planner also asks representatives from the public works, police, and fire departments to serve as advisors on behalf of the town. All meetings will be public, and people who are not on the committee will have the opportunity to speak during open commentary periods. Through painstaking work before the first meeting, everyone agrees to the common goal of outlining a mutual concept for the site through six months of meetings. The planner also clarifies that an agreement among stakeholders will not bind the town, but will serve as a foundation for any development proposal.

To facilitate, the planner now shifts her attention from designing the process to managing the committee. How can everyone be heard without allowing the loudest participants to polarize the group? How should the meetings be organized to encourage civility and to ensure constructive and effective deliberations? How can the developer be engaged productively to consider new ideas while steering her away from being defensive? All these questions must be answered for in-person deliberations in a collaborative process to be effective.

This chapter provides guidance on how to facilitate collaborative deliberations among diverse stakeholders. Deliberation has three phases: *the beginning*, when groups form and establish norms, scope, and focus; *the middle*, when groups clarify their interests, gather technical information, and explore options; and *the end*, when groups narrow the options, package components of a solution, and strive to reach agreement (see figure 1.3). Some simple processes tackle all three phases in one or two meetings. Other processes may stretch out over months or years, such as in the case of developing and implementing a long-term, regional-scale plan.

## THE BEGINNING PHASE

At this phase, participants with diverse views clarify how they will work together to address the problem at hand. Because these conversations are typically divergent in nature, they help to generate many new ideas and options. In these initial interactions, it is important to establish a tone and expectations that will promote collaborative behavior to increase the likelihood of a successful process and a satisfying outcome. This is particularly important in complex, multiparty cases where the players may have a wide range of interests, values, abilities, and knowledge of the issues.

Managing the beginning of deliberation lays the foundation for the tasks to be completed in the middle and end phases. Here are several activities for process managers to pursue at this point.

- Decide who will act as facilitator.
- Establish norms of behavior and ground rules.
- Balance confidentiality and follow open meeting laws.
- Clarify how decisions will be made.
- Create effective meeting agendas.
- Use logistics to improve the chances of success.
- Select the proper role for public officials.
- Deal with parties reluctant to participate.
- Engage the traditional and new media.

### Decide Who Will Act as Facilitator

Collaborative processes work better when someone manages the interactions among the participants. This person can be called the process manager, facilitator, or mediator. Depending on the circumstances, this person can be one of the participants or can come from the outside. The entire group must be involved in the selection process. If the facilitator is forced on the group, the chances of successfully reaching an agreement will be greatly diminished.

## Establish Norms of Behavior and Ground Rules

As the facilitator, the Discordia planner is concerned about how people will behave at the first meeting because the prior public meeting was very heated. She knows that if the first committee meeting is a repeat of the public hearing, the adversarial behavior will likely hinder the progress of collaboration.

Establishing behavioral norms is one of the first crucial steps in any collaboration if a group is to reach agreement. Agreed-upon norms will help the participants establish expectations of appropriate behavior. Discussing and adopting ground rules or process protocols is the first step in establishing norms. If the group cannot agree on ground rules, a collaborative process might not be possible at that time.

Ground rules can be simple or complex. In private land use mediation cases, basic ground rules address confidentiality, the role of the facilitator, and the role of participants. In public processes, ground rules usually address who can speak when, for how long, what kind of behavior is expected of participants, how agendas will be handled and by whom, who has decision-making authority, and how decisions will be made. Ground rules may also describe the role of different participants, media participation and behavior, how meetings will be run, and how to record meetings.

At the first meeting of the Discordia Mall committee, the city planner proposes ground rules for participants to discuss. Her goal is to help the group establish behavioral norms early. She is likely to face one or two common reactions to the ground rules. One is indifference: the participants may not pay much attention to the ground rules and will have to be reminded of them. The other common reaction is that people may be offended by seemingly being treated like children. In this case, she will have to reiterate why guidelines are important to shift the dynamics of interaction from oppositional to problem solving. She should then help the group revise the rules until they are acceptable to everyone.

Ground rules may be as simple as a few key principles or several pages long, describing a whole set of conditions, expectations, roles, and responsibilities. In either case, the following principles are often included in ground rules.

- **Be respectful (avoid personal attacks).** Ground rules center on the basic notion of civility. The planner/facilitator asks people to avoid personal attacks, to feel free to express themselves, and to disagree without being disagreeable. If any of the participants is hostile or overly aggressive, it can derail the whole discussion and prevent participants from working together.
- **Share the floor (do not grandstand or dominate).** At the hearing, many people speak with concern, clarity, and brevity. However, a few people treat the public hearing as a forum for their personal views, speak at too great a length, and escalate their own emotions as well as those of others.
- The planner has several ideas for handling situations in which a few loud people dominate. First, she states that the citizen's role in democracy is not just a right, but also a responsibility. She asks people to agree that everyone has the right to speak and everyone has the responsibility to listen. Using round-robins and name placards are options that are discussed in the section on surfacing interests.
- **Be patient and persistent (stay at the table even when it is uncomfortable).** The facilitator wants to ensure that if participants come to the workshop, they will stay to hear each other out. She is particularly concerned about how the developer will react if the conversation is difficult. Of course, the planner cannot single out the developer at the meeting, but she can speak with her between meetings confidentially. The planner/facilitator can also say to the group, "As long as we agree to expectations of basic civility, we also need to agree that everyone will be patient and persistent, and will stay in the conversation however uncomfortable it becomes. We will learn a lot more if we make our way through difficult moments."
- **Avoid surprises (keep everyone informed early and often).** Trust will erode quickly if any of the parties withholds information that later comes out as new or damaging information. It is important for the planner/facilitator to stress that, in the spirit of collaboration, all

parties must share information that might be important, unusual, or have an effect on the process.

- *Come prepared (do your homework).* The facilitator asks participants to review summaries of past meetings, the agenda, and any documents sent out ahead of time. She agrees to be timely in her correspondence with the participants prior to the meetings and in return asks that participants come prepared so committee meetings can be substantive and productive.

---

**Box 6.1**

**Sample Ground Rules for Meetings**

- One person speaks at a time.
- Make an effort not to repeat what has already been said.
- Avoid toxic language.
- Focus on the future.
- Speak for yourself, not for others.
- Come prepared.

---

## Balance Confidentiality and Follow Open Meeting Laws

Many collaborative land use processes are conducted in the open. However, cases can span the spectrum from very public to completely confidential. When land use mediation is conducted under the auspices of a court, the rules are generally set by the court. To participate in a court-annexed mediation, typically a party must have standing in the underlying lawsuit. Often these conversations are confidential.

In public policy disputes that are not subject to litigation, there are numerous options from fully public to semiprivate to constrained (Baker 2011). Some processes may be completely public, with laws requiring that people are notified in advance of each meeting and that all meetings are open to everyone. In more constrained cases, the participants could be limited to direct abutters, the proponent, technical experts, or the city planning staff. In these cases, the facilitator or sponsor must carefully review the law. Are these meetings considered public? What open meeting laws apply, who participates, and under what conditions? What confidentiality can be promised by the mediator and the parties, given state mediation statutes? Answering these questions will depend on the open meeting laws in each state and the type of decision that is being made. It is important to address these questions early in the process to put in place the appropriate provisions for openness or confidentiality if necessary.

---

**Box 6.2**

**Questions to Answer About Confidentiality and Open Meeting Laws**

- Do local, state, or federal laws require the meetings to be open to the public?
- If not, is it important for the meetings to be open to the public, or are there good reasons to make them private?
- Will meeting notes be prepared, and if so, by whom? Will statements be attributed to individuals in those notes?
- Who can speak about the process while it is ongoing and what are they allowed to report?

---

## Clarify How Decisions Will Be Made

This decision rule, or how a group will determine outcomes, is inextricably linked to the intent of the process. For example, voting with the majority (50 percent plus 1) is a common decision rule. Other options might be super majority (e.g. two-thirds majority), unanimity (everyone must agree), or unanimity minus one.

As noted in chapter 5, the intent of a collaborative process can be to inform, advise, or decide. If the intent is primarily to inform, then decisions rest with the convener, be that a planning agency, city council, or developer. In this case, the overall intent of a mutual gains process would be modest: to seek input and interaction, but would not require a set of recommendations from or an agreement among the parties.

If the intent of the process is to advise, then the decision rule becomes more important. In an advisory process, the convener agrees to take the group's advice seriously and gives participants the opportunity to meaningfully influence the outcome by articulating broad, shared opinions. However, the convener does not commit to following the advice in part or in full.

When the intent is to reach an agreement, it is important to clarify and negotiate early in the process specifically what will constitute an agreement. This will set the bar for the definition of success. Such decision-making processes may commit participants to certain responsibilities, such as agreeing not to oppose the final approach or fully supporting the final approach with their constituents, the public, and the media.

## Create Effective Meeting Agendas

Often meetings begin with a long technical presentation of the facts (such as current zoning regulations, wetlands and storm water laws, or traffic impact and intersection ranking studies) in an effort to get everyone on the same page. This approach assumes the conflict is principally driven by a substantive misunderstanding among the stakeholders. This is rarely the best way to start a collaborative process. Instead, it is much more effective to begin by letting participants talk about the issues that matter most and by setting up processes to gather relevant information.

In the Discordia case, the planner/facilitator wants the tone and format of the committee meeting to be different from those of the initial public hearing. She wants people to feel comfortable and relaxed, and to engage in conversation in which they share their concerns and listen carefully to those of others.

She resists the urge to begin the meeting with presentations. She recognizes that there is confusion and misunderstanding, but beginning by focusing on technical issues will not stimulate dialogue, increase trust, or actually clarify issues for worried or angry people. Instead, she establishes the agenda and objectives for the first meeting.

In consultation with the participants, the planner/facilitator develops an agenda that provides time for reviewing the ground rules. In this way, she is building a process around the needs of the stakeholders, not around technical issues or her own perspective.

There are many methods to begin an effective first meeting. The planner/facilitator pinpoints the issues people care about using techniques, such as small group discussions or a "sticky wall" that enables people to post their written concerns and ideas on pieces of paper. Then she works with the participants to organize into categories the results of their brainstorming. She may suggest starting with a round-robin discussion in which participants, one by one, express their views without interruption for two minutes. She might ask participants to ask one question at a time and require those with multiple questions to wait to ask their second questions to ensure that everyone has a chance to ask a question. For very large groups of 50 or more, she might ask people to deliberate in smaller groups prior to raising issues or comments to the full group. She might assign people as they arrive to ensure that participants are not sitting with like-minded allies. Finally, the facilitator might have the developer produce a set of posters with the site plan, natural features, current traffic patterns, and other information for participants to view informally in smaller groups. These approaches encourage more personal conversation before the difficult issues are raised with the large group.

**Sample Agenda for First Meeting**

- Define and agree on ground rules.
- Articulate the issues of concern.
- Help identify the interests (not just positions) of different parties.
- Begin to change the tone of participants' interaction.
- Develop a rough work plan for the next two workshops.

## Use Logistics to Improve the Chances of Success

In addition to a thoughtful agenda, well-managed logistics can also help ensure a successful meeting. Actions as basic as choosing an appropriate meeting location, time of day, and room layout can help set the tone. If a group of people are overheated, hungry, physically uncomfortable, or unable to see or hear the group well, they are unlikely to produce good results.

In order to signal that this collaborative process is distinct from the required decision-making process, the Discordia city planner/facilitator decides not to hold the committee meetings at town hall. Rather, she identifies a local school with a large room with tables and chairs that can be moved. She can organize the meeting around smaller, comfortable tables rather than use a classroom or auditorium (with rows of chairs facing a stage). She thinks that a typical classroom format sets up an us-versus-them approach with the participants in the audience and the convener in front of the room. She also appreciates that the school has a nearby bus stop for people taking public transit and a parking lot to accommodate those who will be driving to the meeting.

The planner consults with a few of the participants to identify a meeting time that would best suit working people. She provides drinks and snacks to ensure people are comfortable. She brings flip chart stands (easels), markers, and big pads of paper to write down issues that arise. She checks the sound in the room to make sure people can hear because she wants to avoid using microphones, which formalize meetings and interfere with free-flowing conversation. However, if the room has poor acoustics, she will provide handheld microphones that a runner can bring to seated participants, rather than ask people to stand at the microphone, which mimics the public hearing structure. After the meeting, she will develop an email list or listserv of the participants, which she will use to keep participants informed. These basic logistics are key elements in creating a mood that can enhance the process.

---

**Box 6.5**

**Logistical Considerations for Meeting Planners**

- What size room do you need?
- Does the space have adequate heating or cooling for the time of year?
- Does the room have windows for natural light?
- What would be the best room set up? (People around tables or in rows? Space for people to socialize? Space for people to meet in small groups?)
- Do you need a PowerPoint projector?
- Do you need microphones and amplifiers?
- What type of food and drink should you provide?
- What meeting materials will you hand out?
- How will you communicate with parties between meetings?

---

### Select the Proper Role for Public Officials

Facilitators must be sure to clarify the role played by public officials. Since government officials often take on many responsibilities (e.g., convener, assessor, or decision maker as described in chapter 4) it is not always clear what function they are performing at different points in the process. Depending on their goals, officials can choose to separate themselves from the process, to observe, to participate, to convene, or even to facilitate.

As mentioned, the Discordia town planner has decided to facilitate the meetings herself. But she also has to determine the role of elected and appointed board members. According to town ordinance, the planning board (appointed) makes a recommendation on these kinds of conditional use permits and the town council (elected) must approve, change, or deny that recommendation as the final decision. Both the planning board members and town councillors are the ultimate decision makers. The planner/facilitator could keep these public officials at arm's length and submit a final meeting summary to them at one of their formal meetings. However, such a report would likely be less informative to these two groups than if they actually took part in the workshops.

One role for public officials is to serve as liaisons between decision-making boards and the stakeholder group. A planning board liaison might be present at all workshops to listen, learn, and report back to the board. That liaison may also answer technical questions about the town's master plan, zoning, or specific ordinances. An elected official might be present to open the proceedings, encourage effective participation, or describe how the town council will view any recommendations that might result from the process. Public officials need to be cognizant of their obligations for transparency under open meeting laws while participating in these processes (Baker 2011).

## Deal with Parties Reluctant to Participate

Sometimes there are so many people who want to participate that it can be difficult to have a productive meeting. Other times the problem is the opposite: How to engage parties who are reluctant to participate? Parties hesitate to participate for many reasons. Some may not have time to attend meetings. Others may not enjoy group work or may dislike situations in which people are likely to disagree. Still others may not be aware that meetings are happening or understand that they are welcome to participate. Some people may have limited mobility and need significantly more time and effort to attend a meeting. Others may not speak the language in which the meeting is held or may not feel truly welcome. Facilitators can manage the process to minimize these obstacles.

In Discordia, the planner/facilitator has such a challenge with the developer who has already been lambasted in a public hearing. What can she do to encourage the developer to participate? The following tools can be used to encourage well-rounded participation by addressing some of the concerns above.

First, the facilitator can help establish solid ground rules that require participants to problem-solve together and to treat each other with civility. This, of course, is easier said than done. But by establishing clear rules, everyone can agree to act in certain ways and to minimize distracting behaviors. Second, good facilitation often helps people believe that the process will be fair and constructive. The facilitator can talk to the developer about how she is going to conduct the meeting, explaining that her job is to work with the more difficult participants to understand and address their concerns. The facilitator can show people, as time goes on, that someone is ensuring the conversation is well managed and not dominated by the loudest people.

Third, the facilitator can structure meeting agendas so that the developer is not only reacting to criticism, but is trying to address problems. She can use diverse presenters, breakout groups, and key discussion questions to ensure dialogue. Fourth, she can remind the parties that the process is voluntary. While the voluntary nature of such processes may make it more difficult to get participation and action, it also binds the parties to a certain informal contract: we all have to behave constructively so that the key parties do not walk away. At the same time, collaborative processes are very challenging, and there should be encouragement to keep people at the table even when the moment or meeting is difficult.

## Engage the Traditional and New Media

Conflict, not collaboration, sells the news. The Discordia planner/facilitator is concerned that the local paper and blogs will emphasize the areas of disagreement even when things are going well. She is also concerned that participants will play to the local reporter, making positional and incendiary statements. What should she do?

Reporting by people who do not fully understand the discussions can be harmful to the process. Misquotes can decrease newly established and fragile trust among parties. Articles that divulge ideas the group has not yet agreed to can set back the process rather than support it. Excluding the media, while tempting, is not advisable. The media should be managed so that the public stays informed of relevant issues.

Although the media will exercise its First Amendment rights as it sees appropriate, the facilitator can work with them to prevent problems. She can give background facts to reporters so they are fully informed. She can open communication with the local newspaper editor to explain the process and her intention to encourage collaboration. She can then contact the editor if she has concerns about how the process is being covered. In addition, she can propose ground rules to the media.

- Stakeholders may be interviewed only at breaks or at the beginning or end of meetings (not during meeting sessions).
- Cameras and other intrusive instruments must be stationary once the meeting begins.
- Participants will speak to the media only on their own behalf and will not attribute views or comments to others.
- Participants will follow the ground rules when speaking to the press.

The media can, in fact, be an important ally in a good process. In the Meriden, Connecticut, downtown planning case, the local paper, through its strong criticisms of the initial planning effort, served as the catalyst for ensuring a more inclusive process. Because of active efforts to include the paper in the subsequent inclusive process, the paper became one of the biggest proponents of the process and the recommendations.

Traditional media formats are just one of the sources of information today; there are digital media sources such as blogs, Twitter, and websites to consider. These pose perhaps a greater challenge for collaborative processes. Bloggers are not bound to professional standards, an employer, or an editor. Democracy, freedom of speech, inaccuracy, and invective can prevail. The ground rules described here are less likely to be effective in the blogosphere.

There are a few ways to harness and manage this challenge. First and foremost, to the extent the budget and expertise allow, collaborative processes should use all of the available Web technologies. Creating a basic website with a project overview, meeting locations, summaries, and agendas will get the word out to the broadest range of people. A more sophisticated website can provide the forum to collect comments and post opinions. Participants can blog to share their views and to engage others who are not active in the meetings. Email lists and listservs can spread the word about meetings and the process. The ground rules can require that participants adhere to the rules in virtual space as well as in person. In addition, postings that do not follow basic rules of etiquette can be deleted.

## THE MIDDLE PHASE

Once stakeholders reach the middle phase, the divergent nature of the discussions should have generated many ideas. Now these ideas need to be evaluated and narrowed. The ground rules established in the beginning phases will help build the trust needed to transition from the divergent beginning to the ending phase when stakeholders converge on acceptable options.

In the middle phase of deliberations, the principal tasks include the following.

- Establish a constructive work plan.
- Surface interests rather than positions.
- Manage first offers.
- Generate innovative ideas.
- Deal with difficult people.
- Build trust.

### Establish a Constructive Work Plan

The principles the Discordia planner employs to develop a single meeting's agenda also apply to developing a good work plan for deliberations over multiple meetings. While collaborative processes are dynamic and must be adaptable to be successful, they also require a timeline, schedule of activities, interim and final goals, and a clear product. Unlike the required development process, where legal requirements dictate the exact sequence and content of each step, collaborative processes require engagement of the parties in scoping the issues and planning the work. Through consulting others, the facilitator decides how to sequence discussion of the issues, information, and interests to increase the chances of agreement. She makes strategic decisions with stakeholder guidance on whether to tackle the easier or harder issues first.

This approach of involving participants in work planning can be uncomfortable for both local officials and developers. Developers, with significant capital at stake, worry that if they do not control the process, they put themselves at increased risk. Local officials worry that the process will get out of control if they do not stick to the required procedures. As discussed in chapter 2, the irony is that by trying to exercise too much control, officials and developers increase conflict and decrease their effectiveness with the public.

Using the results from the assessment and the first meeting, the Discordia planner/facilitator and the small group plan a series of meetings, select key issues, share information, and generate options. A few key principles should guide the development of the work plan.

- *Keep topics open*. Deliberations are iterative. While specific issues may be narrowed or tentatively agreed upon, the process allows the range of options to remain on the table to ensure the possibility of trading across options.
- *Explore how issues are connected*. The work plan ensures that the parties can move between issues, circling tighter and tighter as the process continues. Good work plans recognize that deliberation is not linear and that parties often need to reach broad, conceptual agreements before seeking agreement on specifics and details.
- *Focus on interests and options*. The work plan should be designed to help the parties surface their interests, not just their positions and demands, and to explore a range of options to satisfy those interests. Adequate time must be provided to allow participants to invent alternatives before deciding on the best options. This enables them to generate ideas for meeting their own and each others' interests.
- *Concentrate on the outcome*. The most effective processes stay focused on the end product, such as a development proposal, draft ordinance, master plan, or neighborhood guidelines. A report, plan, or written document, once agreed upon, needs to become a reality as discussed in the chapter on implementation. Effective processes include discussion

of likely implementation challenges, so participants can prepare for the realities ahead.

## Surface Interests Rather than Positions

Several decades of negotiation research across business, international diplomacy, and government areas have identified that a key factor to successful negotiation is the ability to identify the interests that motivate the positions of the parties. Positions are similar to demands; interests are the reasons behind the demands. Several interests can motivate a position. The difference between interests and positions is discussed in detail in chapter 1.

Most standard public hearings are designed to solicit positions: for, against, and in between. But they are ineffective at teasing out the under-lying interests, concerns, and nuances of the parties who have come to testify. Effective collaborative processes help parties better articulate and jointly explore potential shared interests. This can lead to the development of new ideas or options that meet those interests in creative, innovative, and integrative ways.

Consider a hypothetical example in which residents of a neighbor-hood are worried about the hours of operation of a new arts center being built in an old armory building. The developer wants to create a vibrant center of music, visual arts, and learning. At the public hearing, most of the people adamantly oppose the project because of the fear of noise, music, misbehavior from late-night concertgoers, and so forth. However, when the parties, at the behest of a local elected official, sit down to discuss the issue, the conversation changes. The neighbors talk about an old night club that kept them up at night, the fact that the developer owns a late-night music club in another part of the city, and about their neighborhood's family-oriented nature. They love that there are very old and very young people in their community and believe that quiet and neighborliness are important. Through a volley of conversation, the group develops several options to meet these interests, including chang-ing the size of the performance space, the hours of operation, the hours of food service, and planning for physical noise barriers. During these conversations, the dialogue turns from confrontation to solving the noise issues and preserving the character of the neighborhood while supporting the new development.

A suite of facilitator tools and strategies can be used to surface and clarify participant interests. Among these are the following.

- *Interviews*. Individual interviews, as noted extensively in the assessment chapter, are a powerful tool to engage parties confidentially, build relationships, and tease out more nuanced views of situations than might be expressed publicly.
- *Small focus groups*. Large public hearings provide a marvelous stage for loud, rehearsed statements. Small groups are less conducive to such rhetoric and encourage participants to talk, deal with one another face-to-face, and explore ideas. It is much harder to lambast a person you disagree with who is sitting right next to you at a table than to do so in an anonymous crowd.
- *Talking circles or round-robins*. The format of public meetings in which speakers are given three minutes and a microphone encourages people to express their opinions with bold, positional language. In smaller groups (of less than 15), participants can be asked to express their interests and concerns one at a time, in a talking circle. Each person who wishes to talk gets the floor for as long as he likes (with the ground rule, of course, of giving other people turns). Microphones are discouraged. Sometimes notes are discouraged too, while at other times group notes are the primary product.
- *Facilitation and deliberative inquiry*. Good facilitators respect all points of view and ask effective questions to find out why people care about the things they want or demand. Because of the neutral and process-oriented role of the facilitator, parties are less likely to be defensive or see hidden motives in the questions and conversation the facilitator initiates than in questions asked by other participants. Facilitators can help people change the focus of the conversation from positions to interests, and can be sure everyone gets a chance to be heard. Facilitators can use open-ended and powerful questions to uncover interests, concerns, and possibilities.
- *Charrettes and other visual and mapping tools*. Future development can be difficult to imagine. Interactive visualization tools, drawings, site plans, and models can help parties visualize what a future project might look like. A visual image, for instance, can be put up on a screen, and someone may react and say, "I hate that plan." When asked, "Why?"

they explain (their interests): "The building is too close to the local stream I care about and it obstructs my ability to take my evening walk along the creek. In addition, if there's no passage through the new development up the hill to Main Street, I'll have to walk all the way around." The "hate" statement is a position. The explanation is a set of interests that could perhaps be met by changes to the proposed plan. Graphic representation of the street, building, or neighborhood provides an opportunity for people to understand more accurately what is being proposed and then to articulate their responses, feelings, and interests.

■ **Instantaneous polling.** Keypad or cell phone polling are electronic tools that allow people to answer specific questions in real time by texting their answers on the phones or typing them on a keypad each person holds. Through keypad polling, everyone in a meeting can participate without having to speak in public. Keypad polling allows the facilitator to ask questions and provides instant feedback to everyone about the range of views in the room. Answers can be cross-referenced to show which groups care about which issues. For example, do business owners object to the project, or is it families with young children? How do people in the vicinity feel versus those who come from other parts of the city? This tool is especially useful in large meetings where some participants might not otherwise speak up.

■ **Polling tools.** With the low- to no-cost tools of Web polling, participants at key moments can be surveyed to reveal preferences, interests, and issues. For instance, one could poll individuals on their preference among three designs on the table. Much like those of instantaneous polling, these results can be used to refine proposals or alternatives, as well as to design more focused agendas for upcoming meetings.

■ **Web-based survey tools.** These survey tools can inexpensively and quickly solicit and organize responses for the full committee to discuss. For processes that might include the input from hundreds of people, new tools are available that allow individuals to post and rank ideas online. While these tools are very useful in engaging the public, generating concrete ideas, and getting a sense of priorities, the ideas that emerge tend to be single issues, such as fixing potholes or increasing public signage.

- *Polling using multiple methods of questioning.* A variety of polling questions, whether via keypad, cell phone, or the Web, can be used to uncover underlying preferences. For instance, if you ask, "Which of the three proposals do you like most," a tally of people's strongest preferences will be revealed. However, this does not indicate what might be a second choice or if they could live with the other alternatives. Polling can ask individuals to indicate their preference, what they can live with, or how they might rank the choices. This, in turn, provides a better sense of where there might be common ground.

## Manage First Offers

In the second meeting of the Discordia Mall committee, the developer presents a revised proposal for the parcel with some changes. She has tried to adjust her original application to meet some of the interests expressed in the contentious meetings. She has established a larger setback from the adjacent stream than required by law and has reduced the overall square footage of the development. She also proposes to pay for a signaled intersection at the entrance to ensure better traffic flow and safety.

But, after looking at her revised drawings, many of the participants once again react negatively. They are surprised that the developer has already made up her mind and is making this offer before everyone has had a chance to fully explore the issues. The developer says that she was just trying to show good faith and make changes to meet the concerns she heard, and that the issues are negotiable.

In general, a few key principles apply to first or early offers.

- *Be patient.* Offers frequently make people retrench into their positions and demands. Offers made too early can lead to counteroffers in an atmosphere of distrust that draws people away from, not closer to, a solution. It is important to start by thoroughly discussing interests and options.
- *Invent without committing.* Good processes allow ideas and options to emerge through taking part in dialogue, engaging with technical experts, and jointly naming and solving difficult problems. Participants need plenty of time to consider ideas and to test them against other ideas before they are asked to make decisions. Participants should be

free to invent suggestions without being held to those ideas prematurely.

- **_Let solutions emerge, not diverge._** In the Discordia case, some parties express strong reservations about a major entrance to the redevelopment that is too close to the school where children cross the street. At first, the developer is resistant to considering a new major entrance. But the parties explore a variety of options, and the developer allows the public to work with her engineer and architect in brainstorming other ideas. It turns out that the developer can actually increase square footage, improve traffic flow to and from the site, reduce runoff to the stream, and increase safety, all at once, by relocating the entrance. This idea emerged by allowing diverse parties to express their interests and, through engagement with the technical team, to jointly consider options that met multiple interests.

## Generate Innovative Ideas

The promise of an effective collaborative process is that the group will come up with innovative and promising new ideas. Parties with different views can apply their collective years of experience, knowledge, and creativity to the problem at hand.

Collaborative processes provide an opportunity to innovate, create, and engage in a way that solves problems of physical space based on the interests, values, and identities of the participants. While the best professional planners, engineers, and architects can technically design a project or a plan, they cannot do it well without the data, interests, and expertise of diverse stakeholders.

## Deal with Difficult People

By the fourth meeting in the Discordia case, the participants start to work well together, agree to basic ground rules, and share their concerns and ideas in a respectful manner. But, at this meeting, a well-known activist who is against all development in this part of the state shows up. He is committed to stopping any industrialization in the state. He raises his hand early, attacks the owner, and declares the process illegitimate because it is not part of the required planning board hearings. A few participants chime in, supporting him, while most of the crowd looks uncomfortable and the developer looks angry.

Effective collaboration is often passionate and heated. It elicits an exchange of strong views in an effort to enhance group understanding. However, some individuals feel their interests are advanced if no agreement is reached. These participants will do everything possible to sabotage a collaborative process before an agreement is reached. Effective collaboration is possible only when the participants can agree to maintain a basic level of civility and respect.

What should the planner do as an effective facilitator? She allows the activist to finish. She then turns to the ground rules posted at the front of the room and reminds everyone of the principles of respect and engagement. She asks the committee if they still agree with these ground rules, first turning to the small planning group. She then turns to the full committee and asks individuals one by one if they agree or would like to modify the ground rules. All the participants but the activist agree to the ground rules they developed in the first workshop. The facilitator directs the participants back to the agenda. The activist stands up, says that the process is a complete sham, and walks out.

There are a number of tools for managing difficult people.

- **Enforce the ground rules.** One of the primary services of a nonpartisan facilitator is to remind people of the ground rules without silencing a particular viewpoint. While many in the crowd may be uncomfortable with someone acting out, they are unlikely to be willing to confront a difficult or angry person. Thus, the responsibility falls to the facilitator, whose role and rules (i.e., the ground rules) are clearly defined up front. While many participants find the initial discussion of ground rules tedious, when the rules have to be deployed in a specific situation, participants become more committed to such rules.
- **Acknowledge the concerns.** While some difficult behavior may be strategic, such behavior is often driven by fear, worry, and feelings of powerlessness. A key tool for facilitators and conveners is to acknowledge the concerns and worries of passionate participants. One goal of an effective collaborative process should be to harness, not stamp out, participants' energy and emotions. Fears and anger cannot be lessened unless they are first expressed and acknowledged.
- **Talk privately.** It can be very helpful for the facilitator or convener to talk with the individual privately. These conversations can be a respectful and

friendly effort to find ways to help that person engage more effectively within the ground rules. This may not always work and can be a challenging conversation. However, it may help both the facilitator and the individual to more fully understand the concern and to brainstorm together about how to address the issue.

- *Account for the emotional intensity of the case.* While the activist is an example of an individual with a particular viewpoint and style, processes must account for people who are scared or angry. If some of the stakeholders are deeply upset (which can be determined in the assessment), more time should be allowed for people to express their concerns and listen to each other before moving to a discussion of options and possible solutions. When people are threatened or frightened, they cannot easily undertake the kind of thinking required for expressing interests, listening to others' interests, and inventing options. When you are angry, hearing a facilitator say "let's get back to the facts" is infuriating and denies the fact that you, as a stakeholder, are angry. Dealing with the fear and emotion first, before the facts, is essential.

- *Separate the gripe from the griper.* Even someone who is being difficult may well have legitimate concerns. It is important, to the extent possible, to look past the challenging tone or behavior to the specific, substantive interest or concern being expressed. Do others agree that this topic might be a real concern? Is the issue being raised something that can be explored and addressed, or might more information on the issue be brought to the table?

- *Analyze and name the problem.* Skilled meeting managers or facilitators can even name the problem, although this course is risky at times. For instance, if someone is adamantly talking about positions and making demands, the facilitator can stop the process and acknowledge what is happening. She can restate the demand or concern as an interest. The facilitator can also remind the group that discussing interests can be more constructive than talking about positions. Though naming the problem or behavior may be very uncomfortable, it may also be an opportunity to help the process change course.

- *Use different process techniques.* Sometimes changes in the process itself can help. For instance, setting up small groups may reduce the intensity of the full public group or plenary session. Using a round-robin where each participant is given time can ensure that all, not just the most vociferous, are allowed to express their views. Using online survey tools between meetings can elicit ideas and issues (and allow people to vent as needed).

- ■ *Engage broader constituencies.* If the above approaches fail, the facilitator or convener might approach others from that constituency and raise the issue of the person's behavior. The facilitator can ask allies of the person if they believe that person is being effective and if that constituency's interests are being met. The facilitator might also say that the current dynamics are not moving the discussion along and that ground rules are being broken. Again, in the spirit of problem solving, the facilitator or convener can ask allies or colleagues how best to improve the situation to get dialogue back on track.

In these difficult financial times, more citizens are questioning government action and its intent, cost, and purpose. Many want vigorous review and clear answers. Some groups have a broader strategy in mind and are taught to actively disrupt processes. Handling this type of difficult participant requires a firm hand and the ability to think quickly on your feet.

## Build Trust

Trust is difficult to gain and easy to lose. In situations where people are skeptical and anxious, seemingly benign mistakes or differences of opinion can turn quickly into major eruptions of emotion and contention. But what does it mean to lose trust in someone? Does it mean that you do not believe what the other person says? Does it mean you expect to be disappointed by someone? Does it mean that you do not think the person's actions and words will match up? Or does it mean that you do not see things as they do? It can be useful to have a framework about trust to enable people to diagnose challenges with trust and make it possible to address them. There are four key elements that, in practical terms, make up trust: expertise, reliability, goodwill, and authenticity as shown in figure 6.1 (Govier 1997).

On one side of the trust equation are expertise and reliability. Does that city planner have the right degree, the right expertise, and do her peers judge her work as competent and capable? In terms of reliability, does a person do what she says? Does she show up on time, deliver products on time, and follow through on commitments?

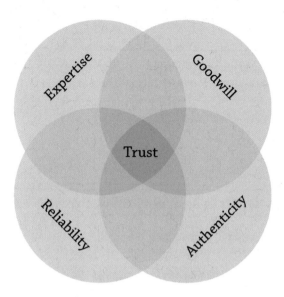

**FIGURE 6.1  Four Components of Trust**

On the other side of this trust equation are intangible, but equally important, factors. Does the person seem to have goodwill and good intentions? Does she listen and generally try to help? Does she share information? Does she admit when she is wrong?

Goodwill and authenticity are not as verifiable. What does it mean to exhibit goodwill? If best professional practice suggests using high-quality materials, but citizens view these as slick, how can authenticity be established? If a developer simply views citizens as generally antidevelopment, how can residents establish trust and engage in problem solving?

There are no simple answers to these difficult questions, but the following are a few best practices for building trust (Conover et al. 2007).

- **Listen, listen, listen.** Proponents of projects too often see their job as trying to convince others (the board, elected officials, and the neighbors) of the merits of their project. They come ready to sell the idea. However, a key skill for planners, project proponents, and consultants is to listen carefully, not make assumptions, and ask questions to deepen their understanding of others' views, concerns, and hopes. Listening to others takes time, patience, and management of one's own emotional and defensive reactions.

- *Avoid surprises*. One sure way to make the journey more difficult is to surprise those who influence the decision making. If proponents make changes, especially in cases where earlier plans set expectations, they should be very clear about how and why. If a press release is planned, let all stakeholders know. If city staff will be moved to another project, let people know when and why. Groups can handle change best if given advance warning and an explanation of why the change is necessary.

- *Talk about the negatives*. Although it is tempting to ignore the negative impacts of a project and to highlight only its benefits, there is no quicker way to destroy credibility than to simply avoid the downsides of a project. To maintain trust, it is particularly important that developers and local officials acknowledge and respond to the problems, risks, and costs to the abutters, the community, or the environment. In this way, stakeholders feel secure that the truth is not being withheld.

- *Talk about the positives*. While the project may have many issues or negative impacts, it has some economic and other benefits for some people in the community. When people focus exclusively on the negative, they may come to be seen as naysayers who oppose everything. It then becomes easy for developers and public officials to discount critics with quite legitimate concerns. Being solely negative diminishes one's effectiveness as a critic.

- *Be prepared to take time out*. When controversy erupts, emotions are high, or limited information about a proposal is available, the stakeholders will need some time to consider. For a project developer, time is money: for every day the project is not built, interest accrues, the market changes, consulting costs go up, and investors grow nervous. However, taking time out to address issues or concerns is time well spent. Consider the realistic possibility of contentious public hearings, slowed political process, and future litigation if angry people are not given the time to sort out the issues.

## THE END PHASE

As the process winds to an end, several challenges will need to be managed. After generating divergent options in the beginning stage and evaluating those options in the middle phase, the stakeholders must converge on a set of satisfactory options. This section provides some guidelines for bringing deliberations to a close by reaching agreement, which include the following.

- Use deadlines.
- Generate packages of solutions.
- Break through impasses.
- Draft an agreement.

## Use Deadlines

Realistic deadlines are important for driving the work to a conclusion. Deadlines can help participants focus and move toward difficult, final decisions and trade-offs. At the same time, arbitrary deadlines that do not have substantive merit may themselves become a subject of dispute. A convener may tell a group of stakeholders that they have six months to come up with new development guidelines or else the town will adopt their own set of guidelines.

## Generate Packages of Solutions

Even for the most engaged and collaborative participants, packaging (or combining) the various components or specific options can be a trying matter. One key task for a facilitator is to clarify the options developed through the process. Throughout the process, numerous ideas will be suggested and considered. At some point, the facilitator needs to ensure those options are captured in writing, graphics, or a drawing. In the Durham, New Hampshire, Mill Plaza case, the three architectural teams were tasked to develop refined conceptual designs for the site. These were presented in drawings and explanations on poster boards for both the advisory committee and public meetings. The conceptual designs were, in essence, packages that involved taking the specific suggestions from previous meetings, the set of principles drawn up by the committee, and the site parameters to create a whole design by each design team. To carry the packaging even further, the "competing" architectural teams were asked to take their best ideas and further combine them into a single, packaged design. The freedom allowed in the advisory committee brought forth the final design.

In Boston's Zakim Bunker Hill Memorial Bridge case, a midlevel engineer recommended putting tunnels under the North Station subway stop winding in and around the Boston Garden sports venue to handle traffic between Storrow Drive and the future Central Artery in a tunnel. Christian Menn, a Swiss bridge designer, put forward the cable stay bridge design that became the Leonard Zakim Bridge, now a Boston landmark. Together, these two key engineering components became the core of a final, preferred package.

If the parties have been able to identify their interests and have agreed upon a set of packaged options, how do they get to a final agreement? How can participants combine the options to reflect the diverse stakeholder interests so that the final project is broadly acceptable, technically well designed, and financially successful? Various components of the decision need to be broken down, options invented, and the pieces packaged in ways to determine which solution is technically feasible, economically robust, and politically viable.

## Break Through Impasses

Toward the end of a process, if parties are exhausted and trust is wavering, the participants may fall back and retrench into their positions. This may create an impasse to reaching agreement. In Discordia, the planner/facilitator has helped the group make progress after working very hard through tough meetings and engaging people at the right time in the right way. But now, the parties cannot move past their differences to a jointly imagined and acceptable solution. When faced with an impasse, process leaders need to focus on ways to alter the conditions in the process, the parties, the expectations, the scope, the time, the implementation, or the risk.

- *Process.* Perhaps the process itself is impeding resolution and needs to be adjusted. The facilitator might begin working with the parties by themselves, shuttling back and forth rather than convening everyone in one room. She might ask for a month-long break from the process to give the parties breathing room.
- *Engagement with the Parties.* The parties themselves are another dimension that might be addressed at an impasse. The facilitator might ask the most vocal participants to allow more reticent people to share their ideas of a package that might be agreeable. The facilitator might suggest that people with differing views talk to each other more

between meetings. Encouraging the group to bring in additional technical assistance may also be helpful.

It may be that the deliberation has become locked and the introduction of new parties—a state official, another neighborhood, more local businesses—might bring fresh energy and ideas to the problem. For example, in a dispute over the treatment of contaminants in groundwater at a military facility on Cape Cod, the responsible, polluting party was at odds with state and federal regulatory agencies on how to proceed (Consensus Building Institute 2008). The community, watching this impasse grow increasingly intense and unproductive, decided to engage a local, well-respected research institution to take a new look at the problem. The research institution's fresh look suggested that rather than paying for more expensive treatment of groundwater, money could be better spent addressing surface water impacts. The research institute concluded that less money spent and more environmental benefit would be the result. This new player, with fresh ideas, broke the impasse. Granted, bringing in players late in the game may require additional education, some backtracking, and alteration of the group dynamic, but if the process is at an impasse, the change may be well worth it.

- *Expectations.* Everyone enters the process hoping they can reach an agreement. However, it may be that the parties can only invent several options or consider a range of alternatives, rather than reach a final settlement. The facilitator might help the parties shift their expectations to a less difficult task. As an example, maybe stakeholders may agree on traffic patterns, but not on what uses are appropriate at the site. Even if the parties do not reach a comprehensive agreement, constructive deliberations can result in final proposals that may better meet the needs of the stakeholders.

- *Scope.* Perhaps parties cannot agree on the large range of issues before them, but could agree on a subset such as traffic patterns, hours of operation, and design guidelines. In this case, the facilitator might help the parties narrow the scope of the deliberations so that parties focus on the areas where they can be productive together. Conversely, it may be that she can help the parties broaden the scope and make it more complex. Sometimes there are just not enough choices to make a deal work. She might find ways to help the parties actually expand the number of issues to consider, which might help overcome the impasse.

- **Time.** Through phasing, breaking large issues into stages, and staggering the start of various aspects in the project, the facilitator might help the parties break the impasse. Could the developer phase in the project over time? Could the developer suggest some initial site work with careful engagement of the community so the citizens can observe how the developer handles concerns such as dust, traffic, and other possible impacts?

- **Implementation.** It may be difficult for parties to come to an agreement before they have discussed how the agreement will be implemented. People need to understand how their work plan will be codified, what their future roles will be, how and when they will be in contact as a group, and if the progress will be monitored. This topic is addressed in detail in chapter 7.

- **Risk.** The final consideration is who bears the risk and how is it managed. For instance, the abutters might fear that the redevelopment will result in excessive traffic. The developer may be equally convinced that through new and advanced strategies, this problem can be prevented or considerably mitigated. The facilitator might help the parties develop a contingent agreement based on the developer's conviction that traffic will not negatively impact those intersections, given the improvements she intends to make. The developer might be willing to take additional measures should future monitoring suggest those intersections have degraded. The abutters can thus be assured that if there is a negative impact, it will be addressed.

## Draft an Agreement

The drafted proposal, agreement, or plan may be a highly technical product (a site plan or architectural rendering), a set of rules or regulations, or a set of principles and guidelines. It is very important for the facilitator to help the parties identify who, when, and what they expect in a final product or agreement.

Who drafts the document can affect perceptions of its legitimacy. Frequently, the answer is obvious. The proponent owes the others a site plan, an approach, or an offer. The city staff drafts new ordinances. However, as our cases have shown, there are many variations to increase trust in and acceptance of the final product. A city may elect to draft neighborhood guidelines before having the developer make a proposal. A proponent may decide to let its consultants (engineers or architects) handle public presentations and share draft products because they may be seen as the most technically proficient. Some technical consultants may be better communicators, and since they are also one step removed from the proponent, skeptics might be willing to trust them.

When participants do not trust one another or when they want someone accountable to their group, they may ask a facilitator, mediator, or independent expert to draft the agreement. Having multiple parties write their versions of the agreement is not advisable. Regardless of the circumstances, the best practice is to develop a single document for all parties to edit or comment upon until it accurately captures the agreement.

# CHAPTER 7

■ ■ ■ ■ ■ ■ ■ □ □

# Implementing Agreements

The Discordia planner has worked diligently with the stakeholders to assess the mall proposal, design an effective collaborative process, and deliberate over the range of options for the site. After reviewing many packages and editing draft agreements, the committee has eventually agreed on a redevelopment plan for the site. With all of this work done, the final step in the mutual gains approach is to make sure that the agreement becomes a reality—that the agreement is implemented.

The solutions identified in the agreement must be converted into an outcome that has the force of law. The stakeholders must remain engaged after an agreement is reached in order to implement it. At this point, however, they are often worn out and ready to return to their lives, but doing so would overlook a critical task. This phase of implementing the agreement is often the lonely orphan of collaborative processes, forgotten until stakeholders realize that something has gone wrong and their vision was not converted into an enforceable outcome. Stakeholders need to advocate for their agreement to ensure the concepts are integrated into the required decision-making process.

The implementation stage ensures that the end product matches the intent of the group. First, stakeholders must incorporate the agreement into a proposal that will be submitted to the decision-making board. Proposals may take the form of a comprehensive plan, the legally binding text of an ordinance, or a very technical and elaborate site plan application to develop a parcel of land. Second, after the proposal is submitted to the decision-making board, the stakeholders must advise the board through participation in public hearings and comment periods in the required process. Third, if the board approves the proposal, the stakeholders must monitor how their agreement is implemented in the outcome. Does the approved comprehensive plan language conform to the agreement? Does the approved ordinance accomplish the goals of the agreement? Does the municipality enforce the approved ordinance? Is the construction of the development following the terms of the agreement?

---

**Box 7.1**

### The Steps of Implementation

- Incorporate the agreement into a proposal.
- Advise the decision makers during the required process.
- Monitor implementation.

---

Once the Discordia Mall committee reaches agreement, the solutions they identify must be integrated into a proposal for the developer to submit to the town. In accordance with the land use laws of Discordia, the proposed redevelopment project requires a conditional use permit (a zoning mechanism that identifies certain uses that are appropriate under the right conditions) that is issued by the planning board. For example, a nursery school may be permitted in a residential neighborhood if certain conditions, such as adequate room for parking, limited signage, appropriate lighting, and screening from neighbors, are met. A municipal board such as the planning board is typically designated to review the permit application and determine if the proper conditions are present. The next step in building the new mall is for the developer to prepare an application that meets all of the specifications of Discordia's conditional use permit ordinance. Once submitted, the planning board will follow the required process before making a decision on the application.

As described in chapter 1, most required processes follow a basic four-stage structure where (1) an application is accepted; (2) it is reviewed by the board; (3) the board and the public comment on the proposal, and adjustments may be made in response to those comments; and (4) a decision is made. If a site-specific proposal is approved, the developer can begin construction based on the conditions imposed by the planning board.

This process of incorporating the ideas in a negotiated agreement into a proposal tends to be unpredictable. Throughout the entire implementation phase, adjustments to the proposal may be made by the developer and the decision makers for a variety of reasons. These changes may be in response to legal requirements that the stakeholders were not aware of, new information that surfaces in public hearings, or changing circumstances that affect the proposal. Stakeholders must be informed of these changes so they understand the reasons for them. If they are not informed and discover that changes were made, they may feel betrayed and may even withdraw their support. If, however, they remain informed of changes to the proposal, they will more likely support the proposal throughout the decision-making process and encourage the decision makers to approve it.

As an example, a group of citizens in Cortlandt, New York, worked for almost six months negotiating the details of the proposed Hollow Brook golf course project with the developer (Nolon 2009; Nolon and Beck 2003). One of the many conditions for citizen support of the development was that the golf course be public rather than private. This condition was part of the initial proposal submitted to the decision-making board. During the required decision-making process, the developer informed the board that the public option for the golf course was no longer feasible. Market conditions had changed and a public course would not bring in sufficient revenue to support the other conditions to which the developer agreed. When he amended the application to make the course private, the negotiating committee cried foul, and most of them withdrew their support for the proposal. For them, having a public course was a significant component of the agreement and they were not willing to support the proposal without it.

If members of the committee had not stayed involved in the approval process, this change might not have come to their attention until after the project was approved. Instead, they were able to voice their objection and convince the developer to make accommodations before a final decision by the board was made. Responding to the group's comments, the developer explained his rationale and negotiated another solution. In the end, they agreed that the course would be open to residents on certain days and remain available for the local school teams. By maintaining communication throughout the required decision-making process—after the collaborative agreement was reached—the parties were able to adjust to new information and amend their initial agreement as it moved into the early phase of implementation.


## THE THREE PRIMARY STAKEHOLDER TASKS DURING IMPLEMENTATION

### Incorporate the Agreement into a Proposal

The ideas in any negotiated agreement must be integrated into a proposal or report upon which the decision-making body will act. In Albuquerque's North 4th Street Corridor case, stakeholders negotiated an agreement that became the basis of a zoning ordinance adopted by the local board. In the Massachusetts Assembly Square case, the parties agreed on how to develop the site and their agreement was then incorporated into an official application for approval by the local decision makers. Planning for the Zakim Bunker Hill Memorial Bridge began in the 1980s as part of the Big Dig, and four lawsuits were filed challenging the proposed bridge design. As discussed previously, a bridge design committee convened in 1991 as a condition of the environmental review. The parties eventually reached an agreement on the design that became a part of the final proposal. The decision makers in the federal and state governments eventually approved the design in 1994.

Depending on the complexity of the negotiated agreement, it may be challenging to integrate the agreement into a proposal that conforms to the board's requirements. For example, a development agreement like that reached in the Assembly Square case has many requirements. The conditions of the agreement must be converted into a proposal with accurately scaled diagrams and the required level of detail. The proposal may need to go through an environmental review process. Additionally, the proposal may need approval from other agencies beyond the principal decision maker. For example, the Discordia Mall redevelopment may need approvals from the state department of transportation to change the patterns of access to the site in addition to the conditional use permit by the planning board.

The challenge at this stage is moving from the conceptual agreement to a specific, approvable proposal or permit that will be submitted to the board. The proponent may draft the proposal alone or in conjunction with the stakeholders, but either way she must consult with the stakeholders during the drafting process. Once the proposal is drafted, there must be a procedure to keep the stakeholders updated on progress and to gather their feedback. In essence, the stakeholder committee members who reached an agreement should become advisors during the proposal-drafting process. They no longer participate as intensively as they did in the negotiations, but they should be kept up to date about how the agreement is being incorporated into the proposal. In some situations, one or two stakeholders may be designated as liaisons to provide status updates to all other stakeholders. A facilitator or the drafter can coordinate this interaction. These lines of communication are critical because new information often surfaces that requires reinterpretation of the agreement. Each deviation may be acceptable individually, but when viewed in the aggregate, it can become objectionable. Keeping this group informed ensures that they will participate as proponents when the required process begins.

### Advise the Decision Makers During the Required Process

Once the proposal is complete, it must be submitted to the appropriate board or agency to initiate the required process. Among the four stages in the required process in figure 1.2, the public has the greatest opportunity to provide feedback to decision makers during the public comment period. During the comment stage, the public voices its support, concerns, and feedback to the board and recommends that the project application be approved or denied. In most significant land use decisions, public comment periods become a battle; proponents argue for approval and opponents plead for a denial. Often the parties attack the substance, they attack each other, and they attack the board.

If the proposal adequately captures the agreement, the public hearing can take on a different function. Instead of being the first opportunity for stakeholders to express their concerns, the hearing is an opportunity for these same stakeholders to endorse the proposal.

Stakeholders' support for a proposal can range from enthusiastic to reserved. For example, during the public hearing for the Woodcrest senior housing project in Mount Kisco, New York, all of the participants attended the public hearing and requested time to speak to the board (Nolon 2009).

One after another, the participants spoke about the benefits of the project, their involvement in the process, and the responsiveness of the developer, and they asked the board to approve the application as submitted. It was so impressive that the developer's attorney, who had not been part of the negotiations, told the developer that he had never seen such enthusiastic support in any of his past land use approvals.

In a Los Angeles land use mediation over the expansion of a college campus into a residential neighborhood, the support among stakeholders was more subdued. While the neighbors felt that their concerns about traffic, aesthetics, and property values had been addressed, they did not feel comfortable speaking in favor of the proposal during the public hearing. As a result, they were unwilling to support the proposal before the city council, but they agreed not to oppose it or appeal if it was approved. In other cases, as a negotiated proposal is presented, some groups who were not involved in the negotiations may criticize the proposal. Even in such cases, an effective collaborative process allows both the proponent and opposition to be heard. The negotiating group can show the decision makers the trade-offs that were made and how the full range of views were incorporated.

## Monitor Implementation

Once the decision-making board adopts a plan, passes an ordinance, or approves a development, the next step is to act on the approval. If the board approves a comprehensive plan, there must be a system in place to see that the vision becomes a reality and that future land use decisions are consistent with the plan. If the board approves an ordinance, the administering staff and agencies must have the resources and commitment to enforce that law. If the board approves a development, construction must follow the requirements of the approval. Therefore, construction is another period when stakeholders, landowners, developers, city staff, and other key people need to track progress and communicate. Monitoring provisions should be discussed in the deliberation stage. The stakeholders should discuss who will track project activities and communicate with the group; how frequently this will be done; and what to do if conditions change or there is an unexpected twist in construction. The stakeholders should consider in advance the conditions under which parties might lose trust with each other and how that might be avoided.

**Questions for Monitoring Implementation**

- Who will track the project activities and progress once the plan is approved?
- Who will communicate with stakeholders or the public, through what mode, and how often?
- What happens if there is a key staffing change?
- Will there be subsequent meetings?
- What will happen if conditions change unexpectedly? What is the plan for discussing that?

A well-designed monitoring program helps to track progress, maintain relationships, and prevent future conflict.

Working out the details of a monitoring mechanism after an agreement is reached, rather than at the time of the agreement, can be difficult. The parties may feel that their work is done and resist efforts to stay involved. They may have different expectations of what will be required of them in the implementation phase. For example, in the Los Angeles campus expansion mediation, the developer assumed that reaching agreement meant that the neighbors would speak in favor of the proposal during the public comment period. The neighbors assumed that reaching agreement meant they would not actively oppose the application during the comment period and would not file a lawsuit after the project was approved. By clarifying this early in the deliberation stage, they avoided a surprise later in the process. The sooner the parties can come to a mutual understanding about what will happen after they reach agreement, the more likely they will be able to implement their agreement.

The parties must have a system to keep track of what is happening and how the decision is carried out. There are many ways to establish monitoring procedures. Formal mechanisms may use designated boards or committees with enumerated responsibilities and clear lines of authority. The mechanisms can be highly structured by designating who will sit on the committee, how committee members are appointed, what procedures will be used to make decisions, and how conflicts will be resolved. More informal mechanisms rely on the relationships of the parties, the resources available, and the type of agreement involved. If the parties have built some degree of trust, they might create a subgroup consisting of representatives from each stakeholder group to periodically update the wider group on the progress and any changes.

---

**Box 7.3**

**Examples of Monitoring Methods**

- Stakeholders who participated in the negotiation of a comprehensive plan can lobby for the plan to be implemented with ordinances. Stakeholders may attend board meetings to make sure the plan is given the full force of law through an ordinance.
- To ensure that a newly enacted ordinance is being enforced, some stakeholders should attend board meetings to monitor how new projects are being processed. This will help determine if the law is being ignored or enforced, and it allows the parties to connect the details of the new ordinance to how the ordinance is actually functioning.
- The developer can email project updates to the negotiating committee. Alternatively, a subset of stakeholders or a representative can periodically visit the construction site to make sure construction is going according to the plan.
- In larger, more complicated development projects, the parties can designate an independent technical professional to ensure that best practices of the industry are being followed to match the commitments in the agreement.
- The project manager or developer can communicate through neighborhood organizations, government agencies, or local clubs such as Rotary or real estate associations.
- An incident reporting system can be established. When certain circumstances occur (e.g., electric power shuts down or dust levels exceed a standard), the incident is reported and made public. Additionally, the response of the developer may be shared widely. The parties can establish a complaint process to raise specific concerns and a protocol for handling those issues.

---

If a project is significant (multiyear, extremely large, and with extensive impacts), a formal advisory committee with clear membership guidelines might be needed to monitor implementation activities. Such a formal mechanism for monitoring would also be appropriate if significant distrust exists among the parties, resources are available to pay for monitoring, and the board decides to approve a development.

For example, in the Los Angeles campus expansion mediation, a highly formal plan was created called the Community Advisory Committee to monitor the construction and use of the facility. The committee's stated purpose was to (1) oversee the implementation of this agreement; (2) monitor the implementation of mitigation measures for the project; and (3) provide an ongoing mechanism for communication between the college and the community to foster harmonious and compatible relationships. The committee was made up of seven members: two selected by the college, two chosen by the adjacent neighbors, two selected from the community at large, and one member from the student body.

The Community Advisory Committee selected a chair to facilitate meetings, contact members, and prepare agendas. The group articulated a specific time frame for meeting and a scope for discussion. They agreed that their decision rule was consensus less one, provided that at least one member from each of the three stakeholder groups was present. In the event that differences of opinion arose concerning the implementation of the agreement, the parties agreed to use a mediator. If agreement was not reached with the help of the mediator, the parties agreed to submit the disagreement to an arbitrator. Selecting both the mediator and the arbitrator required a consensus. They also created penalties for frivolous or bad-faith referrals to the mediator.

Monitoring tasks will vary drastically depending on the type of land use decision. Monitoring the implementation of a comprehensive plan or local ordinance will require a different commitment than monitoring a site plan or subdivision development decision. Comprehensive plans are implemented through the adoption of ordinances, bylaws, and/or regulations, which are in turn adopted through the local approval process. For example, if a comprehensive plan calls for increases in affordable housing, a local law must be enacted to convert that vision into an enforceable standard. Once the law is passed, a local approval board must enforce the requirements through individual landowners when they submit proposals. Those watching to ensure commitment to the original agreement need only attend local hearings, read meeting minutes, and follow the type of applications that come before the approval board. Monitoring those activities takes commitment, but not sophisticated technical capabilities.

Monitoring a development proposal, on the other hand, presents a very different set of circumstances from monitoring the implementation of a comprehensive plan or enforcement of an ordinance. A decision to approve a development project is implemented through the construction of that project. Depending on the nature and scope of the agreements, the conditions may be easy or very complicated to monitor in the construction process. For example, commitments to suppress dust by keeping access roads wet are easy to monitor. On the other hand, committing to use low-phosphorous fertilizer on a golf course requires costly monitoring procedures. In situations demanding complex monitoring, adequate resources must be set aside to ensure compliance.

Typically, monitoring detailed and lengthy conditions falls to someone on the municipal staff, such as the town planner. However, limited funds and time allocated to planning departments hinders their ability to carry out these tasks. It can be a great help if participants agree to assist with monitoring. Some governments can require developers to pay for third-party monitoring.

## FACTORS AFFECTING IMPLEMENTATION

Several factors influence whether an agreement will be implemented as written.

### The Stage When Implementation is Introduced

The groundwork for a successful implementation effort should be laid in the earlier stages of collaboration. At this time, likely implementation obstacles or challenges should be considered and a draft plan for implementation activity and monitoring should be drawn. Decisions about who will monitor construction and how it will be communicated may be a part of the assessment process. During process design, the planning team, facilitator, and convener might explore options for the type of implementation they envision. During the deliberation stage, parties can agree on the specific mechanisms for implementation. In this way, the seeds for successfully implementing an agreement are sown at the very beginning.

## The Subject Matter

The nature of the proposal plays a big part in whether an agreement can be implemented as discussed. Planning and zoning matters may be harder to implement than site-specific development projects. Proposals to adopt a new comprehensive plan or enact a new zoning ordinance present implementation challenges because the issues are more numerous and nebulous (traffic, housing, commerce, infrastructure, aesthetics, natural resources, and community character); stakeholders may be hard to identify and engage; and time frames are likely to be longer. Implementing comprehensive plans and ordinances takes place over many years and many decisions.

Site-specific development proposals, on the other hand, can be easier to implement because the issues are more clearly defined, stakeholders more identifiable, time frames shorter, and the legal, decision-making structure simpler. For example, in a negotiation over the expansion of the J. P. Carrara gravel mine in East Middlebury, Vermont, the potential stakeholders were limited to a handful of residents who lived nearby (Nolon 2012). Issues such as noise, dust, traffic, groundwater, and property values may be numerous and significant, but addressing them is more manageable because the stakeholders are identifiable and the impacts are limited to what happens on the parcel. Are the developers following the work schedule? Are the roads being watered down to reduce dust? Have groundwater monitoring wells been dug? Have water tests been completed?

## Sustained Support

Converting the plan or agreement into binding law and then monitoring requires energy, resources, and commitment on behalf of a variety of governmental officials, staff members, project proponents, stakeholders, and community volunteers. Because the length of development is often measured in years (and in large-scale development, sometimes decades), ongoing institutional and structural means to ensure compliance are necessary because many parties involved in the original agreement may leave the community or turn their attention to other matters.

## Changing Political Climate, Economics, Staffing, and Priorities

Agreements are made at a specific time, with specific participants, under specific laws and policies, and with a particular group of elected officials at the local, state, and federal levels. They are made in a context of the existing local or regional issues at that time. These conditions will not remain static. An election may occur, economic conditions may improve or deteriorate, new environmental concerns may come to light, and community groups may form or disband. Process designers need to be aware of the unique circumstances of each situation and avoid the temptation to inflexibly stick with a formulaic approach. Each situation deserves tailored attention.

## RECOMMENDATIONS FOR EFFECTIVE IMPLEMENTATION

### Design the Process Well from the Beginning

At this point, it may seem obvious that early stages of a collaborative process affect the later stages. If the process design is inadequate (e.g., the right people are not at the table, the process is not adequately transparent, or it is not endorsed by the decision makers), the parties will have a harder time reaching and implementing an agreement. Process choices that leave important stakeholders feeling disenfranchised and disappointed with the outcome may lead them to intervene and prevent implementation of an agreement in which they were not involved. A bad process is much worse than no process because it takes time and energy, distracts parties from their initial work, builds up hope for a result that may not be possible, and may lead to exploitation. Poorly designed processes can be used to squelch dissent and bury important issues. Co-opted stakeholders can unknowingly legitimate unfair decisions, and the impact may not be recognized until it is too late.

### Discuss Implementation Early

The importance and challenges of implementing the agreement must be discussed with the participants throughout the process. Stakeholders need to take the time to consider implementation challenges that may arise and decide early on how to best address them.

## Keep Lines of Communication Open
## Throughout Implementation

Once an agreement is reached and the implementation plan is being carried out, the stakeholders must be regularly informed of the progress. Email, blogs, wikis, social networking sites, and other technologies provide useful vehicles to maintain communication and monitor progress. Through a combination of electronic and face-to-face communication, stakeholders can be kept abreast of how their agreements are being realized. In today's fast-paced world of multiple technologies, people expect rapid, almost instantaneous, information through these means.

## Clarify Roles, Responsibilities, and Timelines

Clearly defining the roles of various parties is part of an effective implementation plan. Who is going to review the proposal to make sure elements of the agreement are incorporated accurately and effectively? Who will attend the public hearings and report back to the stakeholders? Who will be on site to ensure that conditions in the agreement and permit are being followed? Timelines are as important in this stage as they are in any collaboration. Stakeholders should know how much time is needed to prepare the application, how long the approval process will take, and how long before the project is developed or the plan is implemented. This information will produce realistic expectations.

## Decide on Consequences

Finally, consequences of not complying with the enumerated conditions in the agreement should be made clear. What happens if the proposal to the decision-making board does not include important conditions of the agreement? What if the board does not issue an approval? What if the stakeholders who promised to endorse the proposal do not show up at the public meeting or, worse, file a lawsuit? What if the parties responsible for completing important tasks fail to deliver? If failure occurs early on, prior to approval, the stakeholders can withdraw their support and actively oppose the application during the required process. After approval, however, an unscrupulous applicant might be tempted to cut corners or a citizen group might file a frivolous lawsuit. The implementation plan can include incentives to perform and consequences of failure or breach.

# PART III CHALLENGES

# CHAPTER 8

■ ■ ■ ■ ■ ■ ■ ■ □

# Resistance and Responses

Despite the many successes of using the collaborative mutual gains approach to prevent, manage, and resolve land use conflicts, many local leaders are hesitant to employ it. When asked to consider a collaborative process or a strategy that involves engaging the public, they can find it tempting to come up with reasons why it is not feasible. This chapter looks at some of the most common reasons for failing to take advantage of mutual gains approaches. In many cases, there is a straightforward response that addresses these concerns. This chapter provides responses in a way intended to be helpful to proponents of effective processes.

The following statements are continuations of the common refrain: *"We can't do that because . . ."*

## OBJECTION 1: THE COLLABORATIVE PROCESS IS NOT PART OF THE REQUIRED PROCESS

Land use decisions must follow the process required by state and local laws in order to be valid and upheld if challenged. An application must be made to a local board and the board must review the application, solicit comments from the public, and finally make a decision. The requirement for a board to follow procedures often leads to several mistaken assumptions. First, many leaders think that the required process limits the board's authority to add new processes. Second, many assume that an additional proposed process would replace the required process. Third, they assume it is not possible to fit different or innovative processes into the required process.

To deal with the first mistaken assumption, we must look at what is actually required by state and local laws. The required process in most communities creates a minimum procedure that must be followed, not a ceiling that limits the adoption of additional procedures. There is a difference between the procedures that must be used and those that can be used, and they are not mutually exclusive.

Local boards can use myriad procedures, including informal site visits and staff consultations prior to the submission of the application to develop. After applications are filed, boards have the flexibility to include additional neighborhood meetings, informal plan discussions, and open public meetings. The board must, at a minimum, use the required process; however, if it feels that additional procedures would be valuable and worthwhile, it can supplement the required process. A host of additional procedures can be integrated into the required process without violating the legal requirements.

Response: *"The required process does not prohibit collaborative processes. It merely defines what is required as a minimum standard for action, not as a ceiling that limits us from doing more."*

■ ■ ■

The second mistaken assumption—that a collaborative process replaces the required process—is common and can be addressed easily. The required process is the rule and must be followed. Those who suggest that a collaborative process would be useful are not advocating that the required process be replaced. Instead, these tools and techniques are intended to supplement the required process, to be used before, during, or after the required process.

Response: *"A collaborative process is not intended to replace what is required. The collaborative process can be incorporated into your required process and is designed to improve your decision and its outcomes."*

■ ■ ■

The third mistaken assumption is that the required process cannot incorporate innovation. Again, this originates in the practice of strict adherence to time frames and procedures required by law. The fact is that most required procedures have more than adequate flexibility to incorporate collaborative techniques. For example, many states allow the required process to be delayed with the consent of all the parties. All states have few restrictions, if any, on preapplication processes (i.e., what can be done before the required process is triggered).

Response: *"The required process has several discrete opportunities where the collaborative process can be integrated legally. For example, the applicant can convene a concept committee to improve the application before it is submitted. Or less formal information sessions at various places and times may be held in addition to the required public hearing."*

## OBJECTION 2: THE COLLABORATIVE PROCESS WILL ADD TIME AND ADDITIONAL HASSLE TO THE ALREADY TIME-CONSUMING PROCESS

From many leaders' perspectives, the final decision will be relatively easy to make and will neatly follow the time frames in the required process. They are unaware of how the process may drag out through appeals after a decision is made. However, the reality is that most significant development decisions do not follow an orderly and timely path. Their complicated and far-reaching nature does not always fit within the confines of the required process and often consumes far more time and resources than predicted. Applicants may have to resubmit revised plans after review by staff. Strong objections by the public may postpone a decision. And, of course, controversial decisions may result in years of litigation and expense.

The first step in dealing with this obstacle is to help the leaders realistically evaluate how long it will take to move from proposal to decision and whether that decision will satisfy all stakeholders. The assessment process described in this book can help decision makers evaluate the time required to implement a mutual gains process. If the leader agrees that the process will take a long time and is not likely to have a satisfying outcome, the next step is to explain how a collaboration will take the same amount of time, yet would likely result in greater stakeholder satisfaction.

The following is an example of a hypothetical conversation.

Process proponent: *Have you considered creating an advisory group to assist with this big proposed project?*

Leader: *No, we cannot add more procedural steps. The applicant already has too many hoops to jump through. Why would we want to add another?*

PP: *Well, it all depends on how you look at it. I do not really see it as adding more hoops, but improving how the project moves through the process.*

L: *What do you mean?*

PP: *How long is it going to take to make this decision?*

L: *Following the time frames in the required process, probably three months.*

PP: *What are the chances of it taking that long?*

L: *Slim to none! Based on how important this decision is to many people, there will be significant delays. It will probably end up taking a year or more.*

PP: *And after that year, when a decision is made, how will the community and the applicant feel about the ultimate decision?*

L: *Probably not great, given all of the compromises that will be made and how much money and time will be wasted to get to that point.*

PP: *What if, instead of spending a year fighting and then ending up unsatisfied, a stakeholders' group is given six months to work with the applicant to come up with a mutually satisfactory plan that could then be submitted to the approving agency? Would that improve the agency's deliberations?*

L: *Possibly.*

Response: "The time that a supplemental mutual gains approach may take must be compared to the costs in time, money, and satisfaction of not engaging in such steps. Furthermore, the period between application submission and a final decision is only the middle of the process of development that also includes the work preceding an application submission and the possible years of delay in court after a disputed decision is made by the local board."

## OBJECTION 3: IT WILL COST TOO MUCH AND THERE ARE NO FUNDS IN THE BUDGET

One advantage of the mutual gains approach is that it improves decision making at the end of the process. A collaborative process might require expenditures earlier than in the required process. In reality, the collaborative process merely shifts to the beginning the costs that would have been incurred defending a controversial decision at the end of the process. In addition, the money is used for a more positive purpose than defending a lawsuit. Investing in these processes builds community and improves civic capacity.

A complicating factor is the source of the money. From a budgeting perspective, the expense of defending against a lawsuit is often allocated not to the decision-making body, but to the legal department, or it is picked up by municipal insurance. Thus, there is an allocation challenge: Whose budget should be used for these supplemental collaborative processes? When proponents of the proposal are willing to pay for additional collaborative steps, this challenge is minimized. Funding of the process is discussed in the assessment and process design chapters. Some cities, such as Albuquerque, New Mexico, have established modest budget line items to fund facilitators when needed. Sometimes academic institutions or nongovernmental planning institutes can help. Foundations can play a valuable role in helping to support such processes. In other cases, multiple stakeholders may agree to provide some funding for the mutual gains approach. Although finding funding takes time and effort, there are multiple ways these supplemental mutual gains processes can be financed.

Response: *"If this is going to be a controversial decision, the municipality will likely spend money defending any decision it makes. Would it be preferable to spend time and money early on in the process to make a better decision or spend that same amount of money later to defend the decision?"*

## OBJECTION 4: WE CAN HANDLE THESE SITUATIONS OURSELVES

Many leaders feel confident that they can effectively manage a controversial proposal. They were elected or appointed to their positions, and managing the process is part of their responsibilities. Supplementing with an additional process can make them feel as though they are failing to fulfill their obligations. However, many leaders are only in their positions for a few years and within that time only a few, significant development decisions need to be managed. The lessons from one project may not shed light on the next project if the same leaders are not in office. This can again limit the potential for a community to learn from past mistakes. In such a case, the unfortunate result is that history is likely to repeat itself.

To explore past decisions, the conversation should focus on what decision was made, not on who made it. Reaching out to convene such a process requires courage and leadership. A regional administrator for the U.S. Environmental Protection Agency, an agency quite familiar with disputes, once remarked that leadership takes the courage to create conflict and the courage to resolve it. Supporting an effective collaborative process requires ongoing political skills to monitor the many interests, develop the plausible alternatives for agreement, and determine how to move the parties toward agreement (and to prepare if a few cannot get there).

Response: *"We are not suggesting that you give up control. You will still be handling this yourself; the ultimate decision-making authority still rests with you and your board. We are suggesting that you lead the disputing parties toward a supplemental process that will be more transparent, will provide more reliable information, will engage the stakeholders constructively to arrive at a more satisfying decision, will reduce or eliminate future litigation costs, and will improve people's confidence in your ability to govern."*

## OBJECTION 5: THE OTHER STAKEHOLDERS WILL NOT PARTICIPATE IN GOOD FAITH— THEY WILL MANIPULATE THE PROCESS

This is a legitimate concern that needs to be addressed. Some stakeholder opposition is based on legitimate, site-related concerns, such as too much traffic, inadequate infrastructure, or change in community character. If these substantive concerns are not addressed, an agreement will not be reached. Other stakeholders, however, might take an opposing view for political gain if preventing a decision will be perceived as a victory. This group will attempt to interfere with any process, be it required or supplemental. The adversarial nature of the required process assists them in their aim because it provides ample opportunity to interfere and disrupt. Political opponents can use time frames and procedures of the required process to promote misinformation, generate fear, construct procedural obstacles, and mount challenges in ways that make the required process very cumbersome.

In contrast, a collaborative process that promotes transparency, inclusivity, and responsiveness is designed to discover and share the underlying concerns of all involved. All stakeholders are invited to raise their concerns. As a result, if one group is using the process to deal with hidden agendas, it becomes evident in a collaborative process and their ability to influence decision making will be limited. Even if some parties remain recalcitrant, a proponent's good-faith efforts to improve the project based on the stakeholder concerns can result in a more satisfying proposal, and one that is more likely to be approved by the board.

Response: *"It is true that there may be people who want to use this approval process to advance unrelated agendas or to slow down the decision-making process. But they will do that regardless of the process you use, and the required process is arguably more beneficial for them because it provides a platform. What if you were able to use a process that engaged a more diverse group of stakeholders, surfaced their underlying interests, and improved a proposal or application so it satisfies a broader range of stakeholders?"*

## OBJECTION 6: HOW DO WE HANDLE PEOPLE WHO DISRUPT THE PROCESS ONLY BECAUSE THEY DO NOT BELIEVE IN PLANNING?

There are indeed people who do not think that planning and regulating land uses are legitimate functions of government. There are also people who initially present this way, but once they are actively engaged, they show an interest in participating and can bring valuable resources to the process. When dealing with such people, the best strategy is to invite them to the table and hear them clarify their goals and interests. This will help determine if they are willing to participate or if they only want to disrupt the process. If, in fact, all they want to do is undermine the process, then steps need to be taken to exclude them from the deliberative sessions so that they do not frustrate the other parties. The legal requirements for inclusion do not apply to the collaborative process, just to the required decision-making process. Revealing their dissident motives will help other people keep such comments in perspective and will provide pressure from the group to limit their involvement.

Response: *"The best thing to do is to invite them to the table so that their true intentions can become known. If disruption is in fact their goal, the deliberative process should be structured so that their involvement is limited."*

## OBJECTION 7: COLLABORATION IS TOO OPEN-ENDED AND AD HOC—WE DO NOT KNOW HOW TO ORGANIZE THIS

These comments voice the common misperception that collaboration is a poorly defined process that will lead to confusion and frustration. By pointing out that a skilled mediator can monitor and manage an effective process, you can introduce the idea that collaboration follows discrete stages with defined tasks. Effective collaboration involves a set of steps and techniques, tested through decades of trial and error, that can increase the probability of a more successful outcome. This concern presents the opportunity to distinguish effective processes from ineffective ones, and to guide leaders to local resources that can locate mediators and facilitators.

Response: *"The mutual gains approach is not an open-ended process. It is a very well-organized and discrete process with a defined set of steps, tools, and techniques that is managed to make the best use of the time and effort the stakeholders put into the decision. We should consult with our local mediation group or center to see what advice they have about how to design a process like this. They have years of experience.*

## OBJECTION 8: WE CANNOT DELEGATE OUR AUTHORITY BECAUSE WE WERE ELECTED AND APPOINTED TO MAKE DECISIONS, NOT TO PASS THE BUCK

In representative democracies, such as the United States, there is an expectation that those in government will carry out civic responsibilities for the rest of us. Many people feel that politicians are elected to deal with difficult decisions in their communities. This expectation works when the decision does not involve long-term and lasting impacts on the community. However, there is a subset of decisions for which citizens prefer that governmental officials seek the public's input as advisors. In these situations, citizens are not asking the government to give up authority to make the decision. Instead, they want greater input and transparency.

Furthermore, the ordinances, laws, and regulations define what land use boards can require when reviewing a proposal. The board's land use authority rarely goes as far as a collaborative process designed to address a wide range of issues raised by stakeholders. Collaborative processes can be used to achieve a more expansive outcome than is often possible through a rule-based process. While the board members retain decision-making authority over the final outcome, they can also shepherd the decision through an inclusive and collaborative process.

Response: *"You will still be the decision maker. You will not be asked to relinquish your decision-making authority to citizens. Instead, you can embrace a process that is more effective at gathering citizen input and evaluating information than the minimal standards of the required process."*

## OBJECTION 9: EVEN IF WE AGREED, WE DO NOT HAVE THE TIME, THE MONEY, OR THE ABILITY TO MANAGE THIS KIND OF PROCESS

This question reveals an awareness of what it takes to conduct an effective process. Because collaborative processes have discrete stages that must be managed effectively, it is advisable to set aside adequate resources and to designate a neutral party with some experience in group decision making and consensus building to manage the process. However, it might take more time if the neutral party is not being compensated for his effort. Money and time are often related. If a process manager is not hired, it will take longer to make a decision and might not produce the desired results. "Garbage in, garbage out" is a useful phrase when dealing with resistance to investing in a good process. Another apt maxim is "go slow to go fast." Taking the time in the beginning to discuss all of the issues and uncover interests will improve the decision making at the end of the process. In numerous case studies, we have found that developers and officials claim that they do not have the time or money for a mutual gains process, but then, in the end, find themselves spending more time and money than they imagined in the required process.

Response: *"That might be true, but we can find someone or some group to manage the process. While it might involve some cost and time, it will be worth it in the end. Wouldn't you rather spend time and money in the beginning to gather information and get people working together than spend that money to fend off challenges to your decision later on?"*

## OBJECTION 10: WE DO NOT WANT TO BE THE GUINEA PIGS WHO TRY THIS OUT FIRST

The mutual gains approach is not experimental. As the case studies in this book indicate, numerous jurisdictions throughout the United States and Canada have used a variety of collaborative processes, from ensuring more satisfying land use decisions to resolving years of contention at the courthouse steps. In *Mediating Land Use Disputes*, over one hundred land use mediations were identified, researched, and analyzed (Susskind, Van der Wansem, and Ciccarelli 2000). Since then, hundreds, if not thousands, of projects have employed mutual gains approaches across the country.

Response: *"There are many successful examples of communities using collaborative processes to handle difficult decisions. While this might be the first time for your community, you can learn much from the experiences of other communities."*

## OBJECTION 11: IF WE USE A MUTUAL GAINS PROCESS FOR THIS PROPOSAL, WE WILL HAVE TO USE IT FOR ALL OF THE OTHERS

Some leaders fear that using a mutual gains process will set a precedent and force them to use it in the future. First, boards are only obliged to use the required process; supplementary processes that they elect for one project do not bind them for future projects. There are many applications that simply do not involve strong concerns or conflicts. In fact, collaborative processes are likely to be the exception rather than the rule, precisely because the existing land use processes are sufficient for many cases. Second, collaborative processes are useful only for decisions where implementation is threatened. Third, if the process produces satisfying results, why would we be concerned with using it again? Some communities and institutions have integrated collaborative processes into their land use decision-making systems to ensure greater public engagement, earlier surfacing of issues and concerns, and less future conflict.

Response: *"Boards are only obliged to use the required process. Using the mutual gains process for one project does not bind you to use it for another. In fact, collaborative processes are not appropriate for most of the decisions that boards make. If you can make a decision that will be implemented by using the required process, there is no reason to supplement that process. The collaborative process is used on a case-by-case basis only when it is appropriate."*

■ ■ ■

Leaders may make a number of objections to the mutual gains approach. Many of the objections are based on legitimate concerns that need to be acknowledged and addressed. It is important to be a smart consumer of collaborative efforts, to choose wisely among process options, and to use them only when they offer a chance to achieve a better outcome than the status quo. At the same time, the status quo cannot be an excuse to avoid innovative and creative ways to address some of the more difficult land use challenges that arise in a community. The supplemental mutual gains process is not theoretical; it has been implemented in numerous jurisdictions, small and large.

# CHAPTER 9

■ ■ ■ ■ ■ ■ ■ ■ ■

## Conclusion: Harnessing the Energy of Disputes

*All polishing is done by friction.*
— Mary Parker Follett

The fact land use decisions cause conflict does not need to be restated. That these conflicts can improve a community does, however, need to be emphasized. Many communities have been rocked by the drama of controversial land use proposals. The intensity associated with these proposals can result in decisions that dilute the benefit to the community and leave those involved in a worse position than when they started. Instead, this energy can be used to improve a community. The path a conflict travels depends on many factors, including who the players are and what is proposed. The decision-making path is one factor that influences all others in the process and the mutual gains approach is designed to pave the way for more constructive management of land use conflicts.

The idea that conflict can be constructive if managed well is not new. Mary Parker Follett, an organizational management scholar from the 1920s, succinctly captured the choices faced when confronting conflict.

As conflict—difference—is here in the world, as we cannot avoid it, we should, I think, use it. Instead of condemning it, we should set it to work for us. Why not? What does the mechanical engineer do with friction? Of course his chief job is to eliminate friction, but it is true he also capitalizes friction. The transmission of power by belts depends on friction between the belt and the pulley. The friction between the driving wheel of a locomotive and the track is necessary to haul the train. All polishing is done by friction. The music of the violin we get by friction. . . . We talk of the friction of mind on mind as a good thing. So in business, too, we have to know when to try to eliminate friction and when to try to capitalize it, when to see what work we can make it do. That is what I wish to consider here, whether we can set conflict to work and make it do something for us. (Metcalf and Urwick 1940, 30–31)

According to Follett, conflict can lead to invention or it can result in destruction. The friction of a land use conflict creates heat caused by a diversity of visions and opinions being expressed. When managed skillfully, that heat can produce a valuable and satisfying result. However, when unmanaged, the heat of friction can burn and erode the core of a community. The mutual gains approach provides a way to manage this friction of ideas to emphasize polishing instead of destroying—to make conflict useful for us.

Engaging conflict constructively requires stakeholders to challenge their tendency to avoid conflict. Instead of avoiding it, developers, local officials, and neighbors should engage each other to explore their differences. In contrast, many developers limit the information they share with the community and try to move through the required decision-making process as fast as possible. These developers quickly discover that avoidance strategies do little to reduce conflict. The friction finds other ways to be expressed—at public hearings, in the media, through political campaigns—that can be very damaging.

Drawing from the wisdom of engagement, we can chart a course that will improve not only how we handle community disputes, but also how we handle disputes at home, in the workplace, and in our governments. To begin, we must recognize that we have a choice when dealing with conflict.

Collaborative approaches increase the opportunity for mutually satisfactory solutions, while rigid, adversarial, rule-based processes reduce those opportunities. That is the choice presented in this book. The small subset of land use decisions that turn into highly controversial conflicts can be managed through either the collaborative mutual gains approach or the rule-based, required process.

Choosing the collaborative mutual gains approach does not mean the interaction will be easy. The aim of collaboration is never to reduce friction but to redirect and manage the energy for a productive use. Collaborative processes are often intense and uncomfortable. Difficult things must be said, trust must be built, and hard choices must be made. But in the end, the friction generated through collaboration is more likely to improve the community than to harm it.

When choosing to replace the adversarial process with a collaborative one, remember the guiding principles of the mutual gains approach and follow the four steps.

## PRINCIPLES THAT INFORM THE MUTUAL GAINS APPROACH TO MANAGING POLITICS, SUBSTANCE, AND PROCESS

After reviewing hundreds of cases over 10 years of research and practice, we have found that the most successful mutual gains processes incorporate the principles discussed in Chapter 1. These principles inform and shape the steps of the mutual gains approach—assess, design, deliberate, and implement—and can be applied to organizing a single meeting or designing a complex, long-term process. While every situation and context requires tailoring and adaptation, the most effective processes incorporate the following principles that warrant repeating.

- Engage early.
- Listen and learn first.
- Build on interests, not positions.
- Design and build an effective process.
- Involve many, not just a few.
- Learn jointly.
- Use a skilled facilitator.
- Build relationships for the long term.

Throughout this book, we show how these principles are used in both real and hypothetical cases. These principles, if followed, steer people away from decision-making traps that lead parties toward adversarial interactions.

They can guide individuals toward productive engagement and away from top-down, minimalistic, and adversarial approaches to public involvement.

## EXPERIENCE AS A RUTHLESS, BUT NECESSARY TEACHER

*Experience keeps a dear school, but fools learn in no other.*
—Benjamin Franklin

The experience of a destructive and unsatisfying land use dispute teaches many community leaders that the required process does little to find common ground among diverse view points. But this lesson alone will not help uncover a better approach the next time around. This book is designed to complete the cycle of learning by providing successful examples of alternative processes. Leaders need exposure to collaborative processes, such as the mutual gains approach, or their ability to learn from experiences will be limited at best. While past experiences can be useful levers when attempting to shift parties' perspectives on process, guiding principles and a road map will also be needed.

Land use conflicts can be long, painful, and difficult to resolve. Many local officials, planners, lawyers, and developers fatalistically assume that all significant land use decisions will tear at relationships and the sense of community. They feel that their only option is the adversarial, trial-like process required by land use laws. However, armed with the knowledge in this book, community leaders can construct a new expectation of decision making that breaks that pattern of division and destruction. The history of broken promises and misinformation need not repeat itself when it comes to land use decisions. The lessons in this book can unlock the path to a new understanding of how local land use processes can engage conflict productively.

## PROVIDING LOCAL GOVERNMENTS WITH SUPPORT

Most local governments do not have extensive resources for training their leaders. Funding is limited and finding qualified volunteers for land use boards can be a challenge. This limits a community's ability to learn from past experiences and take advantage of helpful innovations. Without additional support from regional, state, and federal resources, improvements in local decision making will be halting at best. In some regions of the country, local governments have received this type of support. In the Hudson Valley region of New York State, regional, state, and federal entities provide a host of services to improve how decisions are made. The same can be said for regions in California, Florida, Maryland, Utah, Colorado, and Oregon, to name a few (McKinney et al. 2007; Nolon 2006).

Our local governments need help to encourage local decision-making innovation. Making the information available through books, white papers, and websites is not enough. Local leaders must be trained and this training must be relevant to their experience. To meet the needs of adult learners, the information about collaborative processes must be delivered in an accessible way. Fortunately, a body of research and years of experience in adult education exist to offer guidance (Vella 2002). Training should create a safe and nonjudgmental environment that

- responds to leaders' experience and needs;
- encourages participation by allowing questions and adjusting presentations in response to those concerns;
- sequences the session topics from simple to complex;
- respects the participants as subjects of their own learning; and
- provides for opportunities to experience the innovations taught.

Past experience shapes and inhibits new learning. Leaders cannot be expected to change their views unless attention is first paid to their existing beliefs and perceptions. Leaders need to be able to integrate new ideas into what they already know if they are going to keep and use new information. Therefore, training must be delivered in the context of the leaders' experience in order to be effective.

Delivering this type of training requires a commitment of resources. The federal government should provide states with the resources to train local leaders so communities may avoid the divisive processes and build capacity for better decision making in the future. Once funded, the states can tailor the training to meet the diversity of needs that exist in their states. Without a coordinated effort, local governments will be left to make awkward advances without the benefit of lessons learned from other communities.

## WHAT IS AT STAKE?

We wrote this book because we believe land use decisions matter and that they shape people's lives physically, emotionally, and mentally. They also affect the way people interact with one another. Much more is at stake than merely improving the outcome of one land use decision. Land use matters because these decisions give citizens and neighbors the most direct and immediate opportunity to influence and interact with their government. There are monthly, if not weekly, opportunities for citizen involvement in land use decisions. Each town has multiple boards and commissions with various land use authorities. As the national and state governments become increasingly unable to solve the hard problems, citizens at the local level can model more problem-solving approaches.

How we handle conflict in our community speaks volumes about who we are as individuals and as a community. There will always be land use decisions where agreement cannot be reached. A developer may want too much or a citizen group may find the impacts too severe. These situations need processes such as public hearings and litigation to make sure the rights of the community and the individual are not being trampled. There are, however, many land use conflicts where common ground can be reached and where the benefits will outweigh the costs. These conflicts need to be handled with methods that supplement the required, rules-based, decision-making process. Recognizing that we have the ability to use various approaches will not only help with land use conflicts, it will help resolve conflicts within our families, our workplaces, and ourselves.

We are not in control of what happens around us, but we are in control of how we respond to the course of events. The polarized nature of political discourse in our nation inhibits our ability to solve problems collaboratively. Although we can try to tune out the voices that emphasize our divisions, we can also change the way we run government at the local level. Each one of us has the ability to encourage effective problem solving in our towns and municipalities.

The good news is that the practice and spirit of problem solving in our communities is alive and well, even though the media often over-reports the negative elements of conflict. For every one of the case studies mentioned in this book, there are many similar situations where community leaders found constructive ways to manage conflict. We encourage you to make these productive outcomes part of your community's narrative, and hope the guidance provided in this book will help.

# ■ ACKNOWLEDGMENTS

This book would not have been possible without the help of many people. First, we want to thank Armando Carbonell and Lisa Cloutier, our colleagues at the Lincoln Institute of Land Policy, for their long-term support. Armando and Lisa have encouraged our work through the research, course development, and writing of this book. In addition, Emily McKeigue provided insightful editorial assistance with seemingly endless energy and patience. The Institute has had a significant role in developing and deepening these ideas, and it has had the patience and perseverance to support our work over many years.

We also want to thank Lawrence Susskind and John Nolon, who were integral in the intellectual foundation of this book. Both Larry and John developed many of the supporting arguments outlined in the book, and they provided guidance and counsel in developing early outlines.

There were numerous coauthors of research papers and publications who contributed meaningfully to our ideas. Lawrence Susskind and Mieke van der Wansem authored publications summarizing research involving over 100 land use cases that employed forms of mediation. Matthew McKinney, at the University of Montana's Center for Natural Resources and Environmental Policy, coauthored the paper "Streams of Land Use Disputes" and is one of our core course trainers at the Consensus Building Institute. Heather Conover coauthored many publications intended for developers and land use professionals about engaging the public. Matt Strassberg and Kate Harvey helped conduct and publish research on land use dispute resolution in Vermont in 2009.

Many others had a role in this book. Several graduate and law student interns helped with case studies and research. They include Angela Gius, Carri Hulet, Joel Knopf, Seyi Olubadewo, Todd Schenk, and Rebekah Smith. We also want to thank the readers who gave feedback to improve drafts of the text, including Rebecca Economos, Chris Klutchman, Matt McKinney, and Shiona Sommerville. Thanks to three of our colleagues at the Consensus Building Institute for their ongoing support: Merrick Hoben, who helped develop and deliver the early courses upon which this book is based; Martha Paynter, who assisted with the graphics and the editing; and Meredith Sciarro, who performed numerous tasks to ensure that all of the final elements were complete. And a special thank-you goes to Peter Ellis, who helped us come up with our title.

Finally, we greatly appreciate the hundreds of community leaders with whom we have worked over the years to test different methods and ideas. In some instances, we prodded them to be courageous and try new approaches, but in many other cases, it was they who inspired us to chart new courses. The work these leaders did was rarely easy, but it was always rewarding. We thank them for their courage, their imagination, and for the prospect of continuing to learn together in the future.

On a personal note, we could not have kept our sanity without the loving support of our partners and families. Ona wishes to thank her parents Kendra and Shep for passing on their love of books and reading; her sister Isa for teaching her about conflict and loving resolution; and her husband Garth for choosing to walk this wild path beside her. Sean would like to thank his family, Andrea, Ian, and Ty, for their understanding and loving support—even in light of the many important events he missed to work on this book. Pat thanks his wife, Thea, and daughter, Willa, for tolerating his absence at many weekend family breakfasts while he continued to write.

# ■ REFERENCES

Alberta Municipal Affairs. 2005. The municipal dispute resolution initiative: Five years of resolving disputes together. Edmonton, Alberta.

Baker, R. Lisle. 2011. Exploring how municipal boards can settle appeals of their land use decisions within the framework of the Massachusetts Open Meeting Law. *Suffolk U. L. Rev.* 44:455.

Benedict, Jeff. 2009. *Little pink house: A true story of defiance and courage.* New York, NY: Grand Central Publishing.

Bordone, Robert C. 2008. Introduction to dispute systems design. Paper presented at Harvard DSD Symposium, Cambridge, MA (March 7).

Brown, David S. 2009. Discounting democracy: Wal-Mart, social capital, civic engagement, and voter turnout in the United States. *SSRN eLibrary* (September 9). http://papers.ssrn.com/sol3/papers.cfm?abstract_id=1398946.

Cash, David, and William Clark. 2001. From science to policy: Assessing the assessment process. Faculty Research Working Paper 01-045. Cambridge, MA: Kennedy School of Government, Harvard University.

Conover, Heather, Paula Green, Patrick Field, Stacie Nicole Smith, and Hal Movius. 2007. Building (and maintaining) consensus as a marketing strategy. *SMPS Marketer* (August): 15, 16, 38.

Consensus Building Institute. 2008. Facilitating a superfund cleanup on Cape Cod. http://cbuilding.org/node/30.

Consensus Building Institute and University of Montana Public Policy Research Institute. 2007. Building capacity to shape the future: Problems and prospects facing western amenity-rich communities and adjacent communities. Paper prepared for the Lincoln Institute of Land Policy—Sonoran Institute Joint Venture (December).

Costantino, Cathy A., and Christina Sickles Merchant. 1996. *Designing conflict management systems: A guide to creating productive and healthy organizations.* San Francisco, CA: Jossey-Bass.

DeFlorio, Josh, and Patrick Field. 2007. Cognitive barriers in the land use planning process. Working Paper. Cambridge, MA: Consensus Building Institute (December 24).

Dover, NY, Zoning Code § 145-62(B). 1999. http://www.ecode360.com/11751654.

Eckholm, Erik. 2007. Inside a jumble of poverty, Texans build a future. *New York Times*, August 27: sec. National. http://www.nytimes.com/2007/08/27/us/27colonias.html.

Field, Patrick, Matt Strassberg, and Kate Harvey. 2009. Integrating mediation in land use decision making: A report on systems of land use mediation in Vermont. Cambridge, MA: Consensus Building Institute. http://cbuilding.org/resource/integrating-mediation-land-use-decision-making-report-systems-land-use-mediation-vermont.

Fisher, Roger, William Ury, and Bruce Patton. 1991. *Getting to yes: Negotiating agreement without giving in.* 2nd ed. New York, NY: Penguin.

Gardiner, NY, Zoning Law § 220-62B. 2008. Procedure for Special Permits (1).

Govier, Trudy. 1997. *Social Trust and Human Communities*. Montreal, QC: McGill-Queen's University Press.

Hess, David J. 2009. *Localist movements in a global economy: Sustainability, justice, and urban development in the United States*. Cambridge, MA: MIT Press.

James Kent Associates. 2012. The discovery process. http://www.jkagroup.com /methods/discovery.htm.

*Kelo v. City of New London*, 545 U.S. 469 (2005).

Kotchen, Matthew J., and Stacey L. Schulte. 2009. A meta-analysis of cost of community service studies. *International Regional Science Review* 32(3):376–399.

Mashaw, Jerry L. 1985. *Due process in the administrative state*. New Haven, CT: Yale University Press.

McKinney, Matthew, Sarah Van de Wetering, and Patrick Field. 2007. *Responding to streams of land-use disputes: A systems approach*. Missoula, MT: Public Policy Research Institute, University of Montana.

McQuillin, Eugene. 2011. *The law of municipal corporations*. 3rd ed. vol. 8 § 25:52. Minneapolis, MN: West.

Meck, Stuart, ed. 2002. *Growing smart legislative guidebook: Model statutes for planning and the management of change*. Chicago, IL: American Planning Association.

Melendez, Steven. 2010. *Far south side communities divided over proposed Walmart*. Medill Reports Chicago. http://news.medill.northwestern.edu/chicago/news.aspx ?id=166043.

*Merson v. McNally*, 90 N.Y.2d 742 (1997).

Metcalf, Henry C., and L. Urwick, eds. 1940. *Dynamic administration: The collected papers of Mary Parker Follett*. New York, NY: Harper.

New Castle County Land Use and Permitting Process. 2009. New Castle County, DE.

Nolon, John. 1986. A comparative analysis of New Jersey's Mount Laurel cases with the Berenson cases in New York. *Pace Environmental Law Review* 4:3.

———. 2006. Champions of change: Reinventing democracy through land law reform. *Harvard Environmental Law Review* 30:1.

Nolon, Sean. 2009. The lawyer as process advocate: Encouraging collaborative approaches to controversial development decisions. *Pace Environmental Law Review* 27:103.

———. 2012. Second best practices? Addressing mediation's definitional problem in environmental siting disputes. *Idaho Law Review* 49:69.

Nolon, Sean, and Emily M. Beck. 2003. Collaborative developments: A report on development approvals achieved through collaboration. Unpublished manuscript, on file with author.

Platt, Rutherford H. 2004. *Land use and society: Geography, law, and public policy*. Washington, DC: Island Press.

Porter, Douglas. 2006. *Breaking the development logjam: New strategies for building community support*. Washington, DC: Urban Land Institute.

Religious Land Use and Institutionalized Persons Act of 2000, 42 U.S.C. §§2000cc (2006).

Reynolds, Osborne M. 2009. *Hornbook on local government law*. 3rd ed. Eagan, MN: West.

Shutkin, William. 2001. A river (and $5 billion in infrastructure) runs through it: Sustainability slouches towards Somerville's waterfront. *Boston College Environmental Affairs Law Review*. http://lawdigitalcommons.bc.edu/ealr/vol28/iss4/6/.

Susskind, Lawrence, and Jeffrey L. Cruikshank. 2006. *Breaking Robert's rules: The new way to run your meeting, build consensus, and get results*. New York, NY: Oxford University Press.

Susskind, Lawrence, Mieke van der Wansem, and Armand Ciccarelli. 2000. *Mediating land use disputes: Pros and cons*. Cambridge, MA: Lincoln Institute of Land Policy.

Telecommunications Act of 1996, 47 U.S.C. § 332 (2006).

*Thrash Ltd. Partnership v. County of Buncombe*, 673 S.E.2d 706 (N.C. Ct. App. 2009).

Tomain, Joseph P. 1989. Land use mediation for planners. *Mediation Quarterly* 7(2):163.

Town of Killingly. 2009. Envisioning Killingly's future: Phase I final report. Borderlands Village Innovation Pilot Project (February).

Tucson, AZ, Land Use Code art. 5.4.1.1 (2004). http://cms3.tucsonaz.gov/files/planning/Complete_LUC_Sept2012.pdf.

Ury, William L., Jeanne M. Brett, and Stephen B. Goldberg. 1988. *Getting disputes resolved: Designing systems to cut the costs of conflict*. San Francisco, CA: Jossey-Bass.

Vella, Jane. 2002. *Learning to listen, learning to teach: The power of dialogue in educating adults*. San Francisco, CA: Jossey-Bass.

*Village of Euclid v. Ambler Realty Co.*, 272 U.S. 365 (1926).

# ■ ABOUT THE AUTHORS

**Sean Nolon** is associate professor of law and the director of the Dispute Resolution Program at Vermont Law School. He has extensive experience in consensus building, mediation, and litigation in commercial, land use, and environmental law. He has trained hundreds of local officials, environmentalists, and developers in New York, Pennsylvania, New Jersey, Connecticut, Utah, and Vermont in land use law and public policy mediation. Sean was the director of the Land Use Law Center at Pace University School of Law and founded the Theodore Kheel Center on Environmental Interest Disputes. In 2007, he received the Honors Award from the New York State Bar Association's Environmental Law Section. Sean holds degrees from Cornell University and Pace University.

**Ona Ferguson** is senior associate at the Consensus Building Institute, where she designs and facilitates meetings on environmental and public policy, and on organizational and strategic planning. Her areas of expertise include public land use and management, public policy conflicts, voluntary collaboration, natural resource management, climate change, Superfund sites, and coastal and estuary management. Ona has an M.A. in environmental management from the Yale School of Forestry and Environmental Studies and is currently a lecturer there.

**Patrick Field** is managing director at the Consensus Building Institute, associate director of the MIT-Harvard Public Disputes Program, and senior fellow at the University of Montana Center for Natural Resources and Environmental Policy. He has helped thousands of stakeholders reach agreement on organizational mergers, realignments, regulations, permits, and other land use issues in the United States and Canada. Patrick is listed on the roster of the U.S. Institute for Environmental Conflict Resolution, the EPA's master contract for alternative dispute resolution (ADR) professionals, and the Massachusetts Office of Collaborative Practice. He is coauthor of the award-winning book *Dealing with an Angry Public* and numerous articles, chapters, and research papers. Patrick holds an M.C.P. in urban planning from the Massachusetts Institute of Technology.

# ■ INDEX

Page numbers followed by *b*, *f*, and *t* indicate boxes, figures, and tables. Page numbers in *italics* indicate photographs.

Timing: decisions about proceeding and, 81–83, 82f; in deliberation phase, 136; and mutual gains approach, 157–158; process design and, 93–94, 108
Trust, building in deliberation phase, 131–132, 132f
Tucson, Arizona, 45

Value creation, as mutual gains approach negotiation concept, 19
Values and identity issues, as source of conflict, 58–59
Vermont Environmental Court, 8

*Village of Euclid v. Ambler Realty Co.*, 6, 31

Wal-Mart, 59
West Chester, Pennsylvania, 22t, 52
Wind Turbine Farm, Manchester, Vermont, 23t, 53, 58, 61, 101
Wise-Use Movement, 33
Work plan, in deliberation phase, 122–124

Zoning ordinances: mutual gains approach, 44–45; required decision-making process and, 31–33; statutory procedures and, 41b

# ■ ABOUT THE LINCOLN
  INSTITUTE OF LAND POLICY

The Lincoln Institute of Land Policy is a private operating foundation whose mission is to improve the quality of public debate and decisions in the areas of land policy and land-related taxation in the United States and around the world. The Institute's goals are to integrate theory and practice to better shape land policy and to provide a nonpartisan forum for discussion of the multidisciplinary forces that influence public policy. This focus on land derives from the Institute's founding objective—to address the links between land policy and social and economic progress—which was identified and analyzed by political economist and author Henry George.

The work of the Institute is organized in three departments: Valuation and Taxation, Planning and Urban Form, and International Studies, which includes programs on Latin America and China. We seek to inform decision making through education, research, policy evaluation, demonstration projects, and the dissemination of information through our publications, website, and other media. Our programs bring together scholars, practitioners, public officials, policy makers, journalists, and citizens in a collegial learning environment. The Institute does not take a particular point of view, but rather serves as a catalyst to facilitate analysis and discussion of land use and taxation issues—to make a difference today and to help policy makers plan for tomorrow. The Lincoln Institute of Land Policy is an equal opportunity institution.

**L LINCOLN INSTITUTE**
**OF LAND POLICY**

113 Brattle Street
Cambridge, MA 02138-3400 USA

Phone: 1-617-661-3016 or 1-800-526-3873
Fax: 1-617-661-7235 or 1-800-526-3944
Email: help@lincolninst.edu
Web: www.lincolninst.edu